BOY'S BOOK OF
SNAKES

HOW TO RECOGNIZE AND
UNDERSTAND THEM

By

PERCY A. MORRIS

CHIEF PREPARATOR, PEABODY MUSEUM OF NATURAL HISTORY,
NEW HAVEN. AUTHOR OF "THEY HOP AND CRAWL"

THE RONALD PRESS COMPANY · NEW YORK

Library of Congress Catalog Card Number: 48-9569 .

PRINTED IN THE UNITED STATES OF AMERICA

TO BOYS AND GIRLS OF THE OUT-OF-DOORS

You will find that this book disposes of many stories about snakes which you may have heard, but which are not true. Instead of this misinformation, it will give you an understanding of their habits that is perhaps even more interesting and is dependable because you know the real facts. Ignorance of these facts has done great injustice to our friendly nonpoisonous snakes, and this book is planned to give you an appreciation not only of their harmlessness but also of their real value. There are venomous snakes, too. The book explains how relatively few in number they fortunately are, but it helps you to recognize the danger of these few.

When you read this book you will learn how to recognize the various species of snakes at sight. You will also learn which ones to protect because of their usefulness to gardeners, farmers, and fruitgrowers, which ones to destroy because they are dangerous to man and other creatures. Here you will find out where to look for the various species—in garden and barnyard, field and pasture, woody places, marshes, and ponds. The colors of each species are carefully described, and their habits (including the way in which their young are brought into the world) are fully explained.

In this book you will also learn how to catch harmless snakes, and how to feed and otherwise care for them as pets. You will find out that it pays to treat them kindly and handle them gently, and you will be told why you should finally set them free and the proper time of the year for doing so. Furthermore, you will learn correctly just what to do when you or someone else happens to be bitten by a poisonous snake, knowledge that may be very important to anyone.

The last part of this book gives an account of the more important poisonous and nonpoisonous snakes of other lands. These are the ones you read about and often see in zoos. The colors and habits of all these snakes are also carefully described.

In explaining all these things, I have tried to write as clearly as

iii

possible, avoiding scientific terms that are sometimes harder to understand than they are helpful. But the facts you will learn here will be thoroughly scientific. It is my hope that reading this book will help you to know snakes better. For if you come to know them, you will better appreciate how valuable to man many of them are. After having studied snakes for many years, I believe that, when you too understand them, you will find them just as interesting as birds, flowers, or any other object or creature in the world.

P. A. M.

New Haven
1948

CONTENTS

ILLUSTRATIONS

BOY'S BOOK OF SNAKES

Chapter 1

WHAT IS A SNAKE?

The class of backboned animals known as *reptiles* includes, besides the snakes, the turtles, crocodiles and alligators, and the lizards, many extinct groups as well, of which the ponderous dinosaurs are perhaps the best known. Like the fishes they have a body that is more or less covered with scales, and they have cold blood. This latter simply means that their blood is usually not much higher in temperature than the surrounding air, which explains why they are generally more active on warm, sunny days and why those forms that live in the northern regions have to go underground and hibernate during the cold weather.

At first thought one is likely to feel a little sorry for the snake. With no legs or arms it appears to be under a most discouraging handicap in the eternal struggle for survival, but in reality the snake needs no sympathy on that score for it is by far the most successful of all the reptiles. Snakes have so adapted themselves to varying conditions that we find species that can climb trees and move about with surprising speed through the interlocking branches, others that make their homes in the water and can dive and swim with such expertness that they are able to catch the swiftest of fish, and still others that burrow underground and lead a more or less subterranean existence. The sea snakes have even gone so far as to develop flattened, rudder-like tails. They spend practically their entire lives at sea, coming ashore only for the purpose of laying their eggs. The great majority of snakes, of course, live on the ground, but all of them can swim, many can climb and a few can burrow to some extent. So we find that the serpent has conquered the elements far better than any of the other reptiles.

With the possible exception of the lizards, which swarm in desert countries, the snakes outnumber all of the other reptiles, and they

3

have also succeeded in penetrating a much larger area of the earth. We find snakes living in most parts of the world, even in the more northern latitudes where no other reptile, except a few of the turtles, would be able to exist. Some of the larger islands are without native snakes, among them the Azores, Ireland, New Zealand, and the Hawaiian Islands.

Snakes vary in size and general appearance as much as creatures of any other group. Some of the giant anacondas are as big around as a husky man's thigh, while the diminutive worm snake may be no larger around than a slim lead pencil. Some of the tree and vine snakes are tremendously elongated, slender, almost cord-like serpents, while many of the poisonous vipers are short, stout, and squat. Some of our common varieties exhibit startling scarlet and yellow bands; many tropical snakes show truly beautiful patterns of rich colors, while other serpents are modestly dressed in somber grays and blacks.

Snakes may be characterized as animals with an elongate body which is destitute of limbs but furnished with a tail. In the majority of forms the underside is flattened, but in some, especially the burrowing forms, the body is quite cylindrical. The snake has curved, conical teeth that are renewed periodically, and it also has cold blood like the other reptiles. The skin is covered with scales and plates. The scales may be smooth or they may be *keeled,* that is, provided with a midrib. The water snakes and rattlesnakes are typical examples of those with keeled scales, while the king snakes and the racers are good examples of the smooth-scaled varieties. The snake has no movable eyelids and no external ear openings.

The snake, then, is totally deaf but has fairly good vision. To make up for its deficiency in hearing the serpent is remarkably sensitive to odors and probably to certain vibrations. The forked tongue that is incessantly flicked in and out is not an organ to "sting" with, as so many people used to believe, but is, rather, an organ to aid the reptile's ability to smell. The delicate tips of the tongue are lightly touched to objects in the snake's path, or even waved in the air, and they carry back minute particles to where they are lodged in two small cavities in the roof of the mouth. These cavities contain delicate sense organs quite unlike anything possessed by human beings.

When we observe a snake gliding over the ground with effortless ease, we are likely to marvel that a creature so lacking in the ordinary appendages for locomotion can make such satisfactory and rapid progress. One of King Solomon's famous remarks had to do with that monarch's inability, among other things, to understand the "way of a serpent on a rock."

SMOOTH SCALES (KING SNAKE)   KEELED SCALES (RATTLESNAKE)

The scales of the undersurface of a snake are enlarged and broadened to form transverse, overlapping plates, with the free edges directed backwards. These are called *scutes,* and since each is overlapped by the one in front of it, they all slip easily over any irregularities of the ground. Many of the thick and heavy snakes, such as the vipers and pit vipers, can crawl in a perfectly straight line by pressing the scutes in portions of their body against the ground and then moving the body forward by muscular action. They do not "walk on their ribs," as is often stated, but the body is propelled forward by moving alternate sections of the scutes ahead, resting them on the ground, and holding them there while the muscles push the reptile forward.

This manner of locomotion, termed rectilinear movement, is characteristic of the thick-bodied venomous snakes when they are prowling. The more graceful snakes, such as the racers, rat snakes, king snakes, and others of the Coluber family are not capable of traveling in this way. They progress by a sinuous movement where each curve of the body is pressed against surface irregularities. Even the vipers use this "serpentine" motion when in a hurry. It is interesting to observe a snake on a sheet of polished glass. Those serpents unable to sidewind may thrash around violently, but with no anchor for the scutes on the body to press against, they make little progress. Sidewinding, which enables a snake to crawl efficiently on a smooth surface, is a specialized manner of quick movement in loose sand that has been developed to a high degree by some of the desert snakes. It will be discussed later in the section on rattlesnakes.

All snakes are carnivorous and in a wild state probably confine themselves exclusively to living prey. Captive snakes can often be induced to accept dead food, even strips of meat, and it is possible that occasionally wild snakes will take advantage of a dead animal if they chance upon one and are sufficiently hungry. Indeed, water snakes have been reported as feeding upon dead fish, but, generally speaking, the snake prefers its food to be alive.

Some snakes are very selective in their diets and feed almost exclusively upon one kind of animal. A good example would be the tiny red-bellied snake which eats little else except slugs, or the queen snake which prefers crayfishes above anything else. For the most part, however, the snakes have a rather wide range of food. Water snakes eat frogs, fishes, salamanders, various crustaceans, and aquatic insects, while the terrestrial snakes feed upon frogs and toads, small birds and mammals, birds' eggs, lizards, and other snakes. Few snakes are really cannibalistic, in that they devour their own species, but a surprising number show no hesitancy about overpowering and swallowing a serpent of another species. Our smaller snakes consume vast numbers of insects and insect larvae, while earthworms form the staple diet of others. It might be pointed out here that the food habits, and particularly the food preferences, of many of our common snakes are but imperfectly known. There is plenty of room here for the keeneyed young naturalist, and a few seasons of carefully kept records of observations noted in your own neighborhood might well add to our knowledge about such things.

The snake's jaws are long and well-armed with sharp teeth which point backwards in the direction of the throat. There are no molars for grinding, and therefore all prey has to be swallowed whole. Except for the varieties where some of the teeth are modified for injecting venom, the only function of the snake's teeth is to seize and hold fast the reptile's prey while it is being swallowed.

To overcome struggling prey snakes have developed several methods of behavior. The poisonous kinds strike their prey and inject a dose of venom. Swallowing is then delayed until the victim is benumbed and helpless if not completely dead. The constricting snakes wrap a coil or two about their prey, which may be a mouse or a bird or another snake, and squeeze it until, by shutting off its breath, it is literally suffocated. The constrictors do not crush their victims until they have broken the bones and reduced their bodies to a pliable, easily swallowed mass, as some people used to think; they merely stop their breathing by a powerful and continued squeeze until the creature is past the struggling stage. Other snakes simply press the mouse or bird against the ground with a loop of their body, and hold it there while swallowing it.

Mammals, birds, and fish are usually seized head first in order that the limbs, feathers, and scales will lie snugly against the body and so offer no impediment while going down. Sometimes a snake, in striking, may obtain a grip on a rodent's leg or side, but it usually works around to the head before starting to swallow unless the victim is very small. Frogs and toads are often taken hind feet first.

The snake's jaws do not form rigid units, as they do in the other vertebrate animals, but are separated at the extreme front by an elastic ligament so that the serpent has four separate and more or less independently movable jaws. The reptile secures a good, firm grip, let us say, on the nose of a rat much larger in circumference than itself. One lower jaw, say the right one, pushes forward for perhaps a half inch, while the other jaws remain fixed. The elastic ligament makes this possible. After the sharp, recurved teeth on the right lower jaw have been imbedded in the head of the rat, the left lower jaw slides up even with its mate, its teeth are imbedded, and then the upper jaws creep forward a little, one at a time. Next the lower left jaw is thrust forward for another half inch, and the whole operation is thus continued, aided no little by a copious flow of saliva, until the unlucky rat has been entirely engulfed, the snake literally crawling over its dinner.

The stretching power of the snake's jaw is truly astonishing, and the skin of the neck and body is also sufficiently elastic to enable the reptile to swallow a creature more than twice its own size. After a really big meal, which may require over an hour to disappear entirely from sight, the snake's jaws may be loose and out of shape for some time, but the serpent apparently suffers no other inconvenience than that of lying in a state of torpor while digestion is proceeding.

Many snakes reproduce by laying eggs, while some give birth to living young. In some cases these latter snakes merely retain the eggs within their bodies until they hatch. Scientists call the egg-laying varieties *oviparous,* and those that produce living young *ovoviviparous.*

The eggs are generally elongate, white or grayish white in color, and are covered with a tough, parchment-like shell. Each egg becomes larger and darker in color as the baby snake develops. The young serpent is provided with a sharp structure on its nose, called an *egg tooth,* with which it ruptures the shell when ready to emerge. This tooth is then lost.

The eggs are usually deposited under rotting logs, in decaying vegetation, or in some other moderately moist location. In the great majority of species the mother takes no interest whatever in the eggs after they are laid, but goes away and leaves them strictly on their own. Some species remain coiled near or even about their eggs for some time, perhaps even until they hatch, but this is probably more for protection than for incubation. Some of the captive pythons have been known to increase their body temperature while brooding eggs, but it is doubtful if a cold-blooded animal can generate warmth enough to aid much in the process. The brooding habit, which is not common, is more likely a protective measure to prevent some roving lizard or rodent from feeding upon the eggs.

EGGS OF THE EASTERN BLACKSNAKE

Upon hatching, the young snakelets are fully able to take care of themselves. The poisonous varieties are equipped with miniature fangs and are capable of administering deadly doses of venom. The constricting snakes are able to overpower prey within the compass of their size, and the other varieties are all well prepared to take up the business of living entirely on their own resources.

A snake sheds its skin three or four times each summer, and these discarded, paper-thin skins are often found about stone piles and weedy corners of stone walls. For a few days before this event the snake becomes listless, its colors turn dull and lusterless, and a bluish white film appears over the eyes. The serpent begins by rub-

bing its chin against a stone or the rough bark of some handy tree
root until the outer skin (epidermis) splits and loosens about the
head, after which the reptile literally crawls out of it, turning it
inside out as it does so. The shed skin is a perfect replica of the

COMMON WATER SNAKE WITH NEW-BORN YOUNG

snake, the most minute detail of the scales being faithfully re-
tained. The new skin, which has formed under the old one, is rich
in color and sheen; a snake never looks so colorful, fresh, and clean
as it does immediately after a skin-shedding episode. Even the eye
sheds its outer covering and emerges clear and brilliant. With the
rattlesnakes a new *ring* is added to the rattle each time the skin is
shed. The cast skin stretches considerably during the process and
is usually several inches longer than the snake it comes from.

As was mentioned earlier in this chapter, snakes inhabit a great many different kinds of territory. Many species are always found in or near bodies of water, while others live in the hot and dry desert country. Some prefer to live in rugged, mountainous territory, and some make their homes in rich prairie lands. Many snakes, of course, manage to get by fairly well in several quite different sorts of location, but most varieties show a clear preference for certain types of country.

For the purposes of this book it was thought best to divide the nonpoisonous American snakes into four artificial groups according to the environment where they are most likely to be found. Thus we shall consider in turn the harmless snakes of gardens and barnyards, of fields and pastures, of wooded country, and of swamps and ponds. This is done without any pretense of classification as to genera or species. In the back of the book the reader will find an index in which all the snakes discussed will be listed in their proper zoological position, together with their scientific names as well as their popular names.

Chapter 2

FALSE LORE OF SNAKES

Since snakes are odd and interesting creatures, a great many stories and legends have been woven about them. The size of some serpents, the deadliness of others, and the life histories and habits of all of them are truly interesting, and in many cases remarkable, but unfortunately a goodly percentage of the above-mentioned stories and legends are sheer fallacy. Probably no other group of animals has had so many wild and fanciful tales written about its various members.

Regarding the matter of size, the longest snake ever reliably measured was a reticulated python from the Malay Peninsula, and it was thirty-two feet long. Competent reptile specialists regard thirty-five or thirty-six feet as about the probable maximum length of any serpent, and a snake even approaching that size would be an extreme rarity. Some authorities believe that about twenty-seven feet represents the maximum size of any modern snake. Yet in many old writings, and even in some of the current *Sunday Supplements,* we read of tropical monsters fifty, sixty, and even one hundred feet long!

These supersnakes always manage to escape capture, or, if they are collected, they shrink amazingly when laid alongside a tape measure! The total length of a skin means little, as the reptile's hide is by nature quite "stretchable," and a twenty-foot specimen can very easily be pegged out as a twenty-five- or twenty-six-foot skin. The reticulated python mentioned above is the largest of all snakes, provided that we consider "largest" to mean "longest." If we consider "largest" to mean "heaviest," the palm would go to the shorter but much stouter South American water anaconda.

The swallowing powers of these huge constrictors have also often been grossly exaggerated. We find accounts of deer (antlers and

12

all!), horses, and even bullocks being swallowed with little difficulty. Actually, the largest of these snakes can manage a goat, an antelope or small deer, or a good-sized pig. Most authorities doubt that any snake could swallow an adult man, believing that the reptile would find it impossible to stretch its jaws over the shoulders, but small children could be devoured and probably have been.

These tales about the great size and eating capabilities of our larger snakes are really simple exaggerations, but many of the stories we hear about snakes are utterly false. Some of them are based upon very weak circumstantial evidence or upon observable habits wrongly interpreted, and some have no foundation of fact whatever.

One of the gems of "unnatural history" is the story of certain snakes' milking cows. This tale is current in nearly every land where they have both cattle and snakes. Here in our own country the culprit selected to blame for this act is a really beneficial little gray and brown fellow that has been given the popular name of milk snake. According to this tale, the reptile enters the barn after dark and steals milk from the cows.

There are many reasons why cows go dry or have a sudden falling off in their milk supply, as every good dairyman knows. In the old days the farmer looked around for something to blame this circumstance on, and decided that it must be thievery on the part of some creature. Noting the common appearance of this particular kind of snake around his barnyard, he placed the blame on it. Didn't he sometimes tie the cow's hind leg while he was milking? Well, if the cow was accustomed to a rope around her leg, she probably wouldn't object to a snake's being entwined in the same place.

This simple solution to the missing milk problem, however, falls down completely when analyzed. In the first place, the snake is not provided with mobile lips, nor does it possess a broad, flat tongue. Since this is the case it would be physically impossible for the reptile to create the suction necessary to draw milk from the cow. Secondly, the snake's jaws are armed with needle-like teeth, and where is the cow, no matter how docile, that would stand quietly by while these jaws were clamped to a tender part of her anatomy? Finally, the stomach of the largest milk snake ever seen would hold no more than a few tablespoons of liquid, so it would take a whole herd of milk snakes, working in relays, to make any noticeable difference in the poorest cow ever milked.

The milk snake is not a milk-fed reptile. It feeds upon mice chiefly, and the only reason it sometimes haunts barns and barnyards is that these are the very best places of all in which to find mice. Instead of stealing the farmer's milk it is really doing him a good turn by helping to rid his premises of destructive rodents.

Another story that never seems to lack for defenders and "eyewitness" accounts is the one whereby a mother snake swallows her young when they are threatened with danger and emits them all as good as new when the danger is past. There are scores of perfectly honest people who are absolutely convinced that they have seen baby snakes rush into their mother's mouth. Perhaps they have, but more likely they saw a brood of newly born snakes scatter quickly in all directions upon being disturbed. Some of them may have disappeared under the old snake's body. The human eye is an organ rather easily deceived, and if the mother snake's mouth was partly open at the time, a very common condition with an adult snake when it is surprised, it may have looked very much as if the tiny snakes disappeared down her gullet.

Herpetologists, men who have spent their lives studying snakes and their habits, are almost unanimously against this story, and they cite several reasons why they consider it extremely improbable. The digestive fluids in a snake are extraordinarily potent; all food is swallowed whole and even the bones are dissolved in a relatively short time. It is argued that a delicate young snake could not endure these powerful fluids for even a few minutes and then emerge as good as new. The act would have very little protective value, as a mother snake would have small chance for either escape or defense if she were burdened with a dozen or so young snakes in her throat. The garter snake, which is often accused of this stunt, frequently has fifty or more young at a time! In the majority of cases whole families would be wiped out simultaneously by the threatening enemy, while if the young snakes scattered, as it is believed they do, only one or two of a brood would probably be captured.

Many of our snakes make a regular practice of eating other and smaller snakes. Witnessing such an occurrence might lead the uninitiated to believe he had seen a snake swallowing its young. It is no uncommon thing to kill a snake in the late summer and find living young inside her, but these are babies about to be born. Few people, in slaying a reptile, bother to determine the vital organs, so such a find could very easily be construed as a snake that had just swallowed its young.

There are so many people who claim to have actually seen a snake perform this act that it is very strange that no modern snake specialist has had the same good fortune. It has never happened in any of the large zoological parks, such as those in Washington, New York, London, or Berlin. Here hundreds of young snakes have been born, and here the mother is confined with her offspring, where she would have every opportunity to perform this trick. In a wild state the mother does not remain with her young for any appreciable length of time.

It is interesting to note that in almost every case persons who report the snake-swallowing act report it as a childhood experience. The writer has talked with six different people who declare they have witnessed the act, and all six recall it as something that happened many years ago. Children usually have vivid imaginations, and what might have seemed vaguely possible as a childhood experience may with advancing years become a fixed certainty in that person's mind.

The writer feels, however, that you cannot entirely discount so many would-be witnesses. He personally believes that the case of the snake's swallowing its young is unproved one way or the other, although he leans heavily on the side of the nonbelievers. The strongest support for believing that it does occasionally occur comes from the writings of an accredited scientist and snake expert. In 1799 P. de Beauvois, in the same publication in which he defined the genus *Agkistrodon* (to which our copperhead belongs), related observing the snake-swallowing act and reporting having seen it that very year. This from a recognized authority on reptiles, and *not* something he recalled from childhood, seems like fairly strong corroboration. But various prizes that have been offered at different times for absolute proof, in some cases amounting to hundreds of dollars, have never been claimed. Perhaps in these days of home movie cameras some enterprising young naturalist may succeed in photographing such an event, but until that day our leading herpetologists are just about 100 per cent skeptical, to say the least.

The old, old tale of the "hoop snake" hardly needs to be discussed. This was supposed to be an acrobatic serpent that took its tail in its mouth, formed a hoop of its body, and rolled merrily along, generally downhill! The snake was credited with having a deadly "sting" at the tip of its tail, with which it lashed out in fury when annoyed. The merest scratch from this weapon meant instant death.

This yarn has been current all over the world, but no person has ever seen a specimen of this snake. It is always someone's uncle, brother-in-law, or grandfather who saw it! Here in this country the southern mud snake is sometimes called the hoop snake because it does have a hard and rather sharp spine at the end of its tail. There is nothing poisonous about this spine, however. The mud snake, which is one of the mildest mannered and gentlest snakes we have, is nevertheless feared by many Southern folks.

Any snake's body is marvelously flexible but it is hardly built for forming a hoop. So we can safely label this particular snake story as a complete myth and relegate it to the long list of fairy tales that were a part of early nature lore.

We have probably all heard, many times, about snakes "charming" their prey. By staring fixedly at a bird or mouse the reptile is supposed to be able to glide to within striking distance, while the unfortunate victim is held incapable of movement as it gazes helplessly into the unwinking eyes of the snake. There are many everyday tragedies in our fields and woodlands that appear superficially to support this theory, but they will not stand up under critical cross-examination.

Every outdoor enthusiast is familiar with the antics of a nesting bird when it is disturbed, particularly one that nests on the ground, such as a bobolink, quail, plover, or song sparrow. If an enemy approaches too close to her nest she will feign a broken wing or leg and flutter helplessly about, right in the path of the intruder, in a frantic effort to divert its attention from her eggs or nestlings. Some mammals, especially the rodents, often depend on their protective coloration when danger approaches. They crouch down, "freeze" in one position, and stay there until the last moment, hoping to remain undiscovered. Sometimes the bird or mouse, underestimating the striking ability of the snake, stays too long. Either of these two very common happenings, with a snake involved as the villain, might very easily convince a witness that the reptile had "charmed" its prey, but this story, too, should be placed with the other "unnatural history" items of earlier days.

The question as to whether or not a snake ever willfully attacks humans can be answered by saying practically never, so far as American snakes are concerned. Often an alarmed snake, in a frantic effort to get away, may advance toward a person, but if that person stands still, the reptile will glide past with no thought of "attacking." None of our poisonous snakes is aggressive; they ask only to be left alone. Some will refuse to grant a right of way and will stand their ground stubbornly, daring you to come on, but most of them have learned the virtue of strategic retreat.

During the mating season (May) large individuals of the common blacksnake will occasionally advance towards a person in a threatening manner and may even strike at a person's knees if he doesn't back up. The serpent is of course harmless, and at all other times of the year is interested only in keeping far away from members of the human race. In rare instances pilot blacksnakes have been similarly accused of attacking persons. With the exception of the erratic behavior of these two harmless snakes on rare occasions, it is believed that no American serpent will go out of its way looking for trouble. Several foreign snakes, notably some of the cobras and mambas, are notorious for sometimes attacking man upon sight.

In this connection there is the story of how a snake's mate will linger in the vicinity, seeking revenge, after one of a pair has been killed. In the late spring and early summer snakes are often encountered in pairs, and it is not at all uncommon to kill a specimen and a little later see another just like it near by. This is a perfectly natural association. The romantic idea that the second reptile is seeking retribution for the death of its lover is sheer fallacy.

In some sections of the South there is a saying that it is next to impossible to miss hitting a snake in the head if the shooter will only hold his fire for a brief period. According to this whopper the reptile is a very curious animal, and when a gun is pointed in its direction the snake will rear up and attempt to look down the barrel. Accordingly, all you need do is to wait for a while, the accommodating serpent will line himself up with your gun sights, and you cannot possibly miss!

Such are a few of the more elaborate fairy tales about our snakes. We might wind up this chapter with a few brief items concerning mistaken ideas about snakes in general. Snakes are never slimy, although that adjective is commonly applied to them. They are cold to the touch, but they are as clean as a new broom handle.

Horsehairs do not turn into snakes! There is a kind of wireworm that has the general build and specifications of a horsehair, and these wireworms thrive in stagnant water, especially in the presence of decaying wood. There is no better place to find them than in the old wooden watering troughs so common in rural communities a few years ago. There was pretty certain to be an abundance of horsehairs around the trough, too, so when a slender, black "hair" was seen wriggling in the water, imaginative folks reasoned that it must be part of old Dobbin's tail come to life. A generation or two ago there were few country boys who had not, in their early years, placed horsehairs in a dish of water, fondly expecting to develop a "hair snake."

Rattlesnakes cannot be kept from a place by encircling it with hair rope. The rattler will crawl over the rope as readily as it will over a tree root. Nor can you tell the age of a rattlesnake by the number of rings on its rattle. The snake gets a new ring every time it sheds its skin, normally about three times a year. After the rattle gets to be fairly long, the end rings are commonly broken and lost. If the initial bulb, or "button," is present, however, you can get a rough estimate of the snake's age by allowing one year for every three rings.

Snakes do not wait until sundown to die. They are completely dead when you kill them, but when irritated their muscles will continue to flex for several hours.

Finally, the forked tongue has no "stinging" powers whatever.

Chapter 3

HARMLESS SNAKES OF GARDEN AND BARNYARD

The Garter Snake

The common garter snake is probably better known to most people than any of our other harmless snakes. Called striped adder, grass snake, and many other popular names, there are several geographic subspecies recognized by herpetologists, but the garter snake in some form ranges over most of the United States except in the very arid regions.

Garter snakes come out of hibernation earlier than most of our other snakes, and in Connecticut it is no uncommon sight to see a few specimens abroad on the first warmish day in March, while there is still plenty of ice and snow in the sheltered parts of the woods. They are quite tardy in going into hibernation in the fall, too, so besides the reptile's relative abundance, we have this snake with us for an extra long season.

The average length of an adult garter snake is about twenty-four inches. Conant*[5] records a specimen from Ohio that measured three feet eight inches, which may well be the record for this species. Colors and markings, which are quite variable, differ somewhat in the various subspecies. Following is a description of the common eastern race, once called by scientists *Thamnophis sirtalis,* but now called *Thamnophis ordinatus.* The ground color may be brown, black, or greenish black. There is a central stripe of yellow extending from just back of the head to the end of the tail, with an additional stripe along each side. In some specimens the stripes are faint or even lacking, and in the latter forms there is usually a series of squarish dark spots arranged in a staggered line on the

* For a list of herpetologists mentioned in this book, and also some account of their publications, see page 175.

20

back, which is flecked with white. The underside is greenish gray
and the scales are keeled.

Garter snakes, which are more or less closely related to the water
snakes, show a marked preference for wet places. Boggy meadows
and damp brushlands appear to offer ideal conditions for this rep-

GARTER SNAKE
Greenish black, with pale yellow stripes.

tile, but it is by no means confined to such locations and is very
commonly encountered in hilly country, in gardens and orchards,
and even in heavy timberland. As a matter of fact a garter snake
is likely to turn up almost anywhere. It is one of the few serpents
that is able to maintain its numbers with fair success in our crowded
communities, and almost any city park of moderate size will support
a few individuals.

The food of the garter snake consists chiefly of earthworms,
tadpoles, toads, frogs, and salamanders, so it is not surprising that
the serpent haunts damp meadows by choice. They may eat young

birds and mammals on very rare occasions. Such warm-blooded creatures have been taken from the stomachs of garter snakes, but they may represent dead animals that the reptile chanced upon while they were still quite fresh and soft and hence easily swallowed. Captured garter snakes have been known to accept freshly killed young mice, but in the wild state it is probable that this snake is satisfied with an almost exclusively cold-blooded bill of fare.

Lagler and Salger (*Copeia*,[7] 1945, page 159) have reported an interesting discovery concerning the garter snake's food habits. They found that garter snakes living in the immediate vicinity of a trout-rearing station adopted the food habits of the typical water snakes and fed largely upon young fish. Examination of stomach contents revealed that young trout constituted about 40 per cent of their food. As a check they captured a number of garter snakes from the same sort of country, along streams and borders of lakes, but *not* in the vicinity of a fish hatchery, and these snakes averaged only 6 per cent of fish in their stomachs. It is interesting to note that even the fish-eating garter snakes invariably sought to escape by land and never entered the water to escape when it could be avoided.

The garter snake is a spunky fellow when first captured, resisting handling by striking swiftly and repeatedly. Unless the specimen is a big one, however, its small teeth can do no more than lightly scratch the skin. It doesn't take the snake long to tire of aggressiveness, as a rule, and a garter snake that has been held for five minutes will usually calm down and accept the situation with good grace. After that the snake concentrates on looking for a way to escape, and is quick to take advantage of any carelessness on the part of its captor. But it is not likely to strike again. Real big fellows, approaching three feet in length, have teeth large enough to inflict a nasty scratch and need to be handled with some respect.

Many snakes possess a pair of scent glands near the base of the tail, and when irritated the reptile is prone to discharge a strong-smelling secretion. The garter snakes are particularly noted for this habit, and a freshly caught specimen has an extremely disagreeable odor after a brief handling.

The garter snake gives birth to living young, a fact which, together with the usually large broods, contributes to the species' continued abundance throughout most of its range. Egg-laying snakes have to contend with the danger of having their eggs destroyed by skunks and other prowlers, but the young garter snakes are able to squirm for safety as soon as they are born.

Littered barnyards are good places to look for snakes.

Mating takes place late in April (in Connecticut), and the young snakes, about six inches in length, are born about the first week in August. Some phenomenally large broods have been reported, including one of seventy-eight. The usual number, however, is from fifteen to forty.

In captivity the garter snake is hardy and easy to care for. It thrives on a diet of earthworms and tadpoles, generally accepting food after the second or third day. The majority of individuals quickly become docile and well-behaved, showing little evidence of annoyance on handling.

The Milk Snake

The milk snake is a rather common species in the northern part of this country, from Maine and southern Canada to Iowa. It occurs as far south as northern Florida. It is a constricting snake, killing its prey by throwing two or three coils of its body about it and

MILK SNAKE
Gray, with reddish brown saddle-like blotches.

squeezing it to death, and it is a member of the king snake group. Like many another well-known serpent, this one has acquired several popular names, a few of which are spotted adder, checkered adder, and house snake.

The average length of the milk snake is about twenty-eight inches, with the largest recorded specimen measuring three feet six inches (Blanchard [4]). The snake is rather slender in proportion to its length, with a relatively small head and a cylindrical body. The color above is dove gray, with a series of large, reddish brown, saddle-shaped blotches, irregular in outline, on the back. These saddles are edged with black, and when viewed from above the snake appears to be reddish brown with narrow gray rings. There are smaller, black-bordered blotches on the sides, alternating with those on the back, and the lower surface is silvery or creamy white, heavily marked with black. The scales are smooth and the usual appearance of the snake, except immediately after shedding its skin, is rather dull and lusterless.

We have seen in Chapter 2 (page 13) that this species has been unjustly accused of milking cows, which is the reason for its common name. The reptile's frequent presence about barns and outbuildings is for a different reason, connected with food it is true, but not with cows or with milk. The snake, which is a great hunter of mice and small rats, finds one of the best of all hunting grounds for these rodents in the immediate vicinity of man's dwellings. Field mice, an occasional bird, as well as other snakes and some insects are also eaten. The milk snake is not so great a snake-eater as most of the other members of the king snake group.*

Barnyards are not the only places where one can find milk snakes, however, although the chances for success may be better in such locations. Milk snakes are likely to turn up in many sorts of territory, either hilly or low-lying, but particularly in swampy meadows where the field mice congregate. The snake is partly nocturnal, if not largely so, and during the day is most likely to be found coiled under a stone or log. When searching about a barnyard be sure to look under the boards and rotting planks that are usually to be found scattered about, for it is in such places that the reptile generally spends the daylight hours.

Milk snakes are not so gentle as king snakes, but they are usually not bad tempered. A freshly caught specimen, even a small one, will strike unhesitatingly, but it generally calms down in a short time and is reasonably well behaved. Sometimes when being handled an individual will reach slowly around, take hold of your hand, and start *chewing!* This deliberate attack, so unlike the sudden strike we commonly expect from a snake, takes one by

---

* The milk snake is a member of the genus *Lampropeltis,* and is technically a king snake, but the name "king snake" in popular usage is reserved for another species.

complete surprise, but the serpent's teeth are too small to do any serious damage. When a milk snake strikes and succeeds in getting a hold on, let us say, one's finger, it usually does not let go immediately, as a water snake or blacksnake does, but commonly retains its grip and starts chewing. This habit is more or less common to all the king snakes.

The milk snake usually becomes fairly tame in captivity. The majority of specimens will permit handling with no fuss or bother. They are not too easy to keep in good shape, however, as most of them stubbornly refuse to eat, even when offered their favorite food—baby mice. One who keeps milk snakes for any length of time generally has to resort to forced feeding every few weeks.

This is an egg-laying species that deposits its dozen or so eggs late in June, commonly under a rotting log or in a decaying sawdust pile. The eggs hatch in September, the young milk snakes being about eight inches long and very brilliantly colored, the saddle-like blotches on their backs being bright red with velvety black borders.

There are four or five subspecies of the common milk snake, covering most of this country except the Northwest. Cope's milk snake is at home in the lower Mississippi Valley. This serpent rarely exceeds two feet in length and is strikingly marked with black, yellow, and red rings which usually do not cross the underside, although in some individuals they go completely around the snake. This reptile is commonly mistaken for the poisonous coral snake. The western milk snake is about the same size as Cope's, and it bears the same colors, with the red bands much narrower. This subspecies occurs from South Dakota to Utah and south to Arizona.

DeKay's Snake

This little dull-colored serpent is one of the commonest snakes to be found in gardens, orchards, and around buildings throughout much of this country east of the Rocky Mountains. It was named in honor of James E. DeKay, a pioneer zoologist of New York State early in the last century.

DeKay's snake seldom exceeds a foot in length. It is a slender reptile, dull chestnut or grayish brown in color, with a paler streak down the back. On each side of this stripe is a double row of blackish dots, alternating with one another. The underside is pinkish white, sometimes a little spotted near the tail. The scales are strongly keeled. The young are born alive in late July, generally

DeKAY'S SNAKE
Dull grayish brown, paler on the back.

from ten to fourteen in a brood, and for a short time they look quite different from the mother. Very young individuals, up to three or four inches long, are dark gray or almost black, with a more or less complete ring of grayish white or pale yellow around the neck. At this stage they could very easily be mistaken for little ring-necked snakes, but the two species are really not hard to distinguish. The ring-neck has a deeper yellow band around its throat and its scales are smooth. Therefore if your specimen has keeled scales and a gray or whitish collar, it is not a ring-neck but a very young DeKay's snake. After reaching a length of about six inches the serpent takes on the color and pattern of its parents.

The favorite home of this little snake is any overgrown stone pile in the weedy corner of some old orchard. Among the grass roots and under the dead leaves it finds plenty of food to its liking, while the friendly stone pile provides an abundance of crevices and crannies that can be used for a safe refuge when needed. Since the snake's food consists of worms, salamanders, snails, and a host of various insects, grubs, and caterpillars, it should be rated as a valuable ally to the gardener.

This is one of the first snakes to be seen in the spring. It comes out of hibernation with the first warm days, sometimes even beating the "early-bird" garter snakes in this respect. During the spring months DeKay's snake loves to bask in the sun, generally selecting for its daily sun bath a bare patch of earth or a flat rock hard by some safe retreat. Later in the summer it is likely to spend most of the day hiding under stones or boards, doing its foraging early in the morning and late in the afternoon.

DeKay's snake, which manages to hold its own fairly well even in thickly settled areas, is one of the most abundant species in many localities. This in spite of the fact that it has more than its share of enemies. Besides man, who kills it for no reason at all, it is fair prey for several varieties of larger snakes, and skunks, hawks, and owls feed upon them regularly. Even house cats, while not likely to eat a DeKay's snake unless pressed by hunger, kill hundreds of individuals every summer.

DeKay's snakes are perhaps the most gentle and inoffensive serpents we have, and no amount of teasing will make one think of biting. They do fairly well in captivity, generally accepting earthworms, meal worms, and small insects after a few days of confinement. It is naturally a secretive snake, however, and will spend most of its time hiding under some object in its cage.

THE RED-BELLIED SNAKE

The red-bellied snake, sometimes called Storer's snake, is a near relative of the one just discussed and is probably often confused with it. This snake is quite variable in color, but the common phase is dull brown or brownish gray with or without a paler streak down the middle of the back. The snake is not quite so long as DeKay's snake, averaging about ten inches. The distinguishing character is the abdomen, which in this species is bright orange or strong pink. Like DeKay's snake it has keeled scales, and the newly born youngsters are dark gray with whitish collars.

This species is not so common as DeKay's snake in most places, but it does occur, more or less, throughout most of this country east of the Rockies. Its habits are about the same as those of DeKay's snake, with the red-bellied snake showing a preference for moist and wooded areas. Its choice of food, however, is less varied, this little serpent apparently confining its diet almost exclusively to snails and slugs.

THE YELLOW RAT SNAKE

The yellow rat snake, or four-lined chicken snake, is a reptile of the Southeast, occurring from the Carolinas to Florida and west as far as the Mississippi River. It is a large and rugged species, averaging between five and six feet in length, with a maximum length of nearly seven feet (Ditmars [8]). The body is nearly cylindrical and the scales are feebly keeled. In color the snake is olive yellow or pale yellowish brown, and there are four darker brown stripes extending the length of the body, two on the back and one on each side. These may be rather indistinct on some individuals and vividly prominent on others. The lower surface is pale yellow.

This snake, which is an expert climber, nearly always ascends into the branches of some tree to digest a meal. In fact the majority of specimens found will probably be in trees. The snake commonly invades barns in search of rats or mice, or enters chicken houses for the same purpose, as well as for young chickens or eggs. In such places they are generally found coiled up among the rafters.

The yellow rat snake feeds upon warm-blooded prey almost exclusively. Rats and mice and similar small mammals probably constitute their chief fare, but partly grown chickens and ducks are gratefully taken when the opportunity occurs. The snake is especially noted as an egg robber. The reptile's superb ability in climbing makes it almost certain that during the nesting season it takes a heavy toll of bird life. Young birds, small mice, and eggs are simply swallowed whole, but larger prey is constricted. The num-

YELLOW RAT SNAKE
Yellowish brown, with darker brown longitudinal stripes.

ber of noxious rodents it destroys over a season more than balances the number of small birds devoured, so on the whole this species should be a welcome tenant in any farming community.

The yellow rat snake is no coward when surprised. It does not get wildly excited, like a blacksnake, but if there is any way of escape it will usually retreat in an unhurried, dignified manner. If cornered it will put up a bold and courageous fight. The head and neck will be raised well off the ground as the reptile faces its enemy, the tail will vibrate rapidly, beating a tattoo on the ground, and if the foe approaches too close, the snake will strike viciously and repeatedly until overpowered.

The majority of specimens become fairly tame in captivity, however, and make good exhibition specimens. They feed readily upon mice and similar small game and are quite hardy in confinement.

YELLOW RAT SNAKE

If there is a forked branch of a small tree in the snake cage the rat snake will spend most of its time between meals entwined on it.

The yellow rat snake lays its eggs in July, usually about two dozen in number. The young snakes are about twelve inches long upon hatching, and they are marked quite differently from their parents. Dull gray in color, with a series of darker blotches on the back, they look very much like young pilot blacksnakes, a species to which the yellow rat snake is closely related. By the time the youngsters are one year old they have put on the characteristic four-lined pattern of the adults.

THE SPOTTED CHICKEN SNAKE

The spotted chicken snake also inhabits the Southland, being found rather sparingly in the South Atlantic and Gulf States, and in the lower Mississippi Valley. Except for its coloration, it is much like the more northerly distributed pilot blacksnake, and is in fact considered a subspecies of that reptile.

The spotted chicken snake, also known as the gray rat snake, gets to be about five feet long. Its color is pale gray with a series of large, irregular, brownish blotches on each side. The underside is yellowish gray, more or less dotted with dark gray near the tail. The scales are weakly keeled.

It will be noted that this coloration resembles very closely that of a young pilot blacksnake, to be described later, so this variety might be called a pilot blacksnake that retains its juvenile markings in the adult stage.

Since the spotted chicken snake is not very common in most localities, there is still much to learn about its habits and choice of food. It is known to be a skilled climber, and presumably has about the same habits as the pilot blacksnake or the yellow rat snake, which is also a close relative.

The snake is a powerful constrictor. It gets its popular name from its fondness for young chickens and eggs, many of the individuals collected being discovered while they are raiding some hen house. The reptile no doubt feeds upon small birds and mammals, and, like the pilot blacksnake, occasionally upon frogs.

THE CORN SNAKE

Many snake fanciers regard this species as the most handsomely marked snake in this country. It may be found from New Jersey to the Gulf of Mexico, and westward in the Mississippi Valley to Missouri. In the South it is known as the red chicken snake and the red rat snake.

An average-size corn snake is just about a yard in length, and the maximum size appears to be just under six feet. It is a relatively slender serpent with a cylindrical body, and is alert and grace-ful in its movements. The general ground color is light pinkish gray, and on the back is a pattern of rather large, bright red blotches, each rimmed with a narrow border of jet black, setting it off spec-tacularly against the pale ground color. Two rows of smaller, less brightly colored spots on each side alternate with those on the back.

CORN SNAKE
Pinkish gray, with rich red blotches.

The markings are quite suggestive of those on a milk snake, and, to the writer at least, a freshly shed corn snake always looks like a milk snake that has been dyed scarlet. As with so many of our other reptiles, old individuals are often faded and duller in tone; the most colorful examples are usually to be found among specimens that are a little more than half grown. Underneath, the corn snake is white, heavily marked with large black patches. The scales are very weakly keeled on the back, while those on the sides are smooth.

This snake is a strong constrictor, winding a coil or two of its body around its prey and crushing it to death before swallowing it. It feeds chiefly upon rats and mice, and during the late summer it commonly haunts cornfields to catch the rodents that are attracted by the ripening kernels. The snake's frequent appearance in corn patches has given it its popular name. It also eats birds and eggs, and being an accomplished climber it no doubt destroys many young songbirds during a season, but the snake's continual warfare against the mouse and rat tribe more than makes up for this.

It is typically a snake of farming areas. It hunts mainly at night and is seldom seen abroad during the daytime, spending the sunny hours resting, either under a log or in the fork of some tree. At just about dusk the corn snake starts on its rounds, which, hardly by coincidence, is just the time that the hosts of rodents begin their nightly activities. This reptile does not hesitate to enter cellars, barns, and chicken coops, or any other outbuildings likely to harbor mice.

The corn snake is rather bolder than most of our harmless snakes, and quite often a specimen will refuse to retreat even when excellent and very evident avenues of escape are present. The snake will not attack, but very commonly a surprised individual will stubbornly stand its ground, assume a rigid attitude of defense, and dare you to come any closer!

The striking colors of this snake have made it a favorite with collectors. Fortunately it is reasonably hardy in captivity, and generally accepts food in the form of mice or sparrows with little hesitation. Many individuals become really tame, but the corn snake cannot be trusted as implicitly as some others, such as the king snakes or the bull snakes.

THE GOPHER SNAKE

The gopher snake, also called the indigo snake, is a large, husky, good-natured serpent that occurs from South Carolina to well into South America. It belongs to a group of tropical snakes that are common in South and Central America. In the United States it is represented by two races or subspecies.

The average length is five or six feet, but extra-large specimens may reach nearly eight feet in length. Dr. Ditmars [8] records a gopher snake seven feet nine inches long. The reptile's color is a deep shiny black, both above and below, with the chin, throat, and sides of the head rusty brown. The scales are smooth and highly polished, imparting a blue-black luster to the snake and giving it one of its popular names—indigo snake.

This serpent is at home in farming areas and open country in general. It is not likely to be encountered in heavily timbered sec-

GOPHER SNAKE OR INDIGO SNAKE
Deep blue-black, rusty on the sides of the head.

C531497 CO. SCHOOLS

tions, nor does it ordinarily frequent swamps and marshes, although it may visit the latter in search of frogs during certain seasons of the year. One of its favorite places of refuge is within the burrow of a gopher tortoise, which accounts for the reptile's other popular name—gopher snake.

Rodents, lizards, and other snakes appear to constitute the main food items of this species, but it will eat birds and eggs and frogs. The snake is not a constricting reptile; troublesome animals are held against the ground with a loop of the body while being swallowed. Captive specimens feed readily, as a rule, and are not at all fussy about what they eat, some individuals even accepting fish, although wild gopher snakes probably seldom if ever resort to a piscine diet.

In eating other snakes the gopher snake does not draw the line at poisonous species, and both rattlesnakes and copperheads are sometimes overpowered and consumed. Feeding experiments indicate that the gopher snake, with a lightning-like stroke, grasps the poisonous snake's head and pins its jaws shut. It then deliberately "chews" its adversary's head for some time or until the victim is so weakened that the subsequent swallowing is a relatively safe and easy matter.

There are few big snakes as mild-mannered as this one. A freshly caught gopher snake will object strenuously for a brief period. Some individuals compress the neck for a few inches so that it is flattened *sideways,* a common habit of some of its South American relatives, and while thus obviously "on edge" the snake may strike. However it takes only a short time, as a rule, for the gopher snake to get over its nervousness and become thoroughly docile.

In some sections of the South where they are regarded as superlative mousers and ratters, gopher snakes are sometimes given the run of the place around barnyards. Such individuals become extremely tame, even allowing themselves to be picked up without the slightest sign of annoyance. The gopher snake, in fact, is generally so gentle in captivity that for a long time it has been a great favorite with showmen and traveling carnivals. The combination of large size and mild disposition makes it both impressive and safe for demonstration purposes.

Surprisingly little is known about the reptile's breeding habits. It is an egg-layer, depositing a small number of rather large, whitish eggs, probably sometime in the late summer.

Chapter 4

HARMLESS SNAKES OF FIELD AND PASTURE

THE COMMON BLACKSNAKE

The common blacksnake is well known to almost every boy who has ever gone berrying or nutting or for any other reason roamed in open fields or brushy hillsides during the summer or early fall. This is the big black fellow that loves to lie in the sun just a few feet from some friendly stone wall. It is a fairly common serpent from southern Canada to Florida, ranging west to the prairie country where its place is taken by a closely related form.

The average length of the blacksnake is about four feet, with large individuals measuring close to six feet. Any blacksnake more than six feet long is almost sure to be a pilot blacksnake, a totally different species which will be described a little later. The color of the common blacksnake is a uniform slaty black above and below, with the underside somewhat paler than the back. Most specimens have more or less prominent white patches on the chin and throat. The scales are smooth, not keeled, and the whole snake has a dull, satiny finish that is in marked contrast to the glossy appearance of the pilot blacksnake just mentioned.

The common blacksnake is a lover of open and dry country, especially sunny hillsides and meadows that are bordered with ledges and underbrush. Take a walk some summer afternoon along the sunny side of a stone wall that meanders up over a rocky pasture, and the chances are that before you have gone very far you will find yourself a blacksnake, coiled contentedly on a flat stone or on a bare patch of earth near the wall. It is not an easy task to capture the reptile, for while it may tolerate your passing by at a respectable distance it is always ready to dart into the stone wall at the first sign of danger, like a black arrow.

37

The blacksnake is an active, alert reptile and throughout much of its range, particularly in the Northeast, it is likely to be the largest snake that is commonly seen. The natural result is that a number of fanciful tales have been woven about this serpent; tales that for the most part bear little resemblance to known facts. Some people will tell you that a large specimen can wrap itself about an

Tall grass around a stone wall in late summer an ideal spot for blacksnakes.

arm or leg and actually squeeze it into a condition bordering on numbness. The truth is that the common blacksnake is not even a constricting serpent, and it lacks the power to squeeze its prey in the manner of the king snakes and rat snakes.

The blacksnake is commonly believed to be a sort of boss among the snakes and the mortal enemy of the rattlesnake. While it will seize and devour a garter snake or any other snake that is small enough to be easily overpowered, it does not go about picking fights with snakes of its own size. You may be sure that it gives rattlers and copperheads a wide berth. A blacksnake would come off a bad second best in a scrap with a milk snake of its own size; the milk snake, being a constrictor, would soon have the blacksnake in a helpless condition.

One of the blacksnake's popular names is "black racer," and this indicates the speed that this serpent is commonly believed to possess. The "racer" is certainly a fast-traveling snake when it is in a hurry,

COMMON BLACKSNAKE
Dull satiny grayish black, paler below.

but it does not have the rocket-like speed attributed to it. Clocking experiments seem to indicate that the blacksnake's top speed is only about six miles an hour, which does not seem very fast. But remember that when darting over uneven ground, around brush, and between stones, the reptile's speed appears much faster than it really is.

There is one tall tale about this snake that is actually true! You sometimes hear that a blacksnake will chase you, and this harmless reptile is probably the only American snake that will! During the mating season, which in the Northeast is in May, large blacksnakes will occasionally advance toward a person in a threatening manner, with the head held high and swaying from side to side. Though this maneuver is purely a matter of bluff, nevertheless in most cases it works admirably well! If, however, you stand your ground, the snake will usually turn tail and beat a hasty retreat. At all other seasons of the year the blacksnake is as timid as a rabbit.

This snake, however, is no coward when cornered, and it will put up a courageous fight until overpowered. It thrashes about and strikes wildly with bewildering speed but not too much accuracy, and in the excitement sometimes even bites itself! In captivity the blacksnake is reputedly more intelligent than most other snakes. It is said to make a good pet in some cases, but my own experience with this species convinces me that at least the majority of black-snakes remain irascible to the end, always ready to strike when the opportunity is offered.

The blacksnake feeds upon a variety of things, including birds and their eggs, small mammals, frogs, small snakes and lizards, and insects. It overcomes struggling prey not by constricting but by throwing a loop of its body over it and pressing it firmly against the ground while swallowing it. Though the blacksnake is a good climber it spends the greater part of its time on the ground, not being so arboreal as the pilot blacksnake. The common blacksnake also swims well, but enters the water only on rare occasions and then probably only when it is necessary to get to the other side of some creek or stream. When hunting, especially in tall grass, the blacksnake generally travels with its head and neck held well above the ground.

The blacksnake reproduces by laying eggs. These are rather elongate, white, and usually number from ten to about two dozen. They are deposited late in June or early in July, commonly under some flat stone on a sunny hillside. The young snakes do not look at all like their parents. They are pale gray in color, with a series of brown saddles on the back and numerous dark spots on the sides. At this stage they look like baby milk snakes but are not so intensely red. During their second summer they grow darker, and the pattern becomes increasingly fainter until eventually they acquire the uniform slaty black of the adult.

The blacksnake does considerable good by devouring field mice and other objectional crop pests, but on the other hand it destroys many songbirds, particularly nestlings, and a great many small snakes and lizards that are themselves valuable to the farmer because they consume vast numbers of harmful insects. Probably, on the whole, this species should be considered economically undesirable, but the individuals are not likely ever to be numerous enough to exercise any marked influence in any given locality. The writer, for one, would hate to see this splendidly alert reptile wiped out. A sunny hillside in New England, with its scattered boulders and sun-scorched huckleberry patches, would not seem complete without its quota of basking blacksnakes.

In the midwestern part of the country, ranging from Ohio to the foothills of the Rockies, we find a blacksnake that differs somewhat from the eastern type. This is a slightly smaller and more slender reptile, seldom exceeding five feet in length, and generally averaging about four. Its upper surface is bluish green or dark olive green, and its lower surface is pale yellow. The scales are smooth and the snake has the same satiny luster as its eastern relative.

This snake goes under the names of blue racer, green racer, or yellow-bellied racer. It is an active, nervous snake, noted for its speed in making a getaway when alarmed. It feeds upon rodents, frogs, small snakes, and lizards, killing its prey in the same manner as does the common blacksnake. In fact the habits of the two snakes are almost identical. Scientists do not regard the blue racer as a separate species of snake, but consider it a race of the common blacksnake.

The Coachwhip

The whip snakes are among the fastest and most agile of our serpents. Long and slender, they are obviously built for speed, being even more streamlined than the racers just discussed. In the East this group is represented by the coachwhip snake, found from

North Carolina south to Florida, and west to Kansas and eastern Texas.

The coachwhip is a large snake, attaining a maximum length of just over eight feet, five and one half to six feet being a fair average. The color is yellowish brown with no stripes or bands. The head and the first few inches of the body are deep brown, sometimes nearly black. The lower surface is pale in color, shading to yellowish toward the tail. An interesting feature of this species is the arrangement of the scales. They are smooth, and over the last half of the snake they give the impression of an old-fashioned braided coachwhip. It is easy to understand, therefore, how this particular serpent received its popular name.

The coachwhip is rather closely related to the common blacksnake. Not being a constrictor, it adopts the same tactics as does the blacksnake in overpowering troublesome prey, holding its victim against the ground with the fore part of its body. The coachwhip feeds chiefly upon rodents and there are plenty of these furry gnawers in the section of the country inhabited by this snake—field mice, deer mice, cotton rats, gophers and ground squirrels, wood rats, and such. Birds and birds' eggs are also eaten, lizards and other snakes are not refused, but the coachwhip does not eat frogs or toads.

The favorite haunts of this snake are in open, dry, sandy country and in the pine barrens so prevalent in the Southland. It is not often encountered in moist regions or heavily timbered areas. The coachwhip is a fair climber, and during the season of nesting it may be seen prowling among the branches several feet above the ground in search of birds. For the most part, however, this is a snake of terrestrial habits.

The coachwhip is a bold and fearless reptile when cornered. Like most of our speedy snakes it will make a dash for freedom if there is any chance for a getaway, but if all avenues of escape are shut off it is ready to defend itself in no uncertain fashion. It is not so excitable as the blacksnake, but will assume an attitude of alert defense and await developments, all the while vibrating the end of its tail rapidly, producing a dry, rattling sound in the dead leaves.

If its tormentor approaches too close, the snake will strike, then move quickly forward and strike again.

As a rule the coachwhip is not hard to keep in captivity. Most individuals accept food within a short time and are moderately hardy. The majority of coachwhips never lose their fierce disposi-

EASTERN COACHWHIP SNAKE
Yellowish brown. The head and neck are darker.

tion, however, and they savagely resent handling as long as they live.

Early in the summer this snake lays a small number of elongate, white eggs, usually less than a dozen. The young snakes, mottled gray and black, do not attain the tawny yellowish brown of the adult coachwhip until their second summer.

This is the only member of the whip snake group living east of the Mississippi River. In the West we find several kinds of these active serpents, none of which approach the eastern snakes in size. The so-called western coachwhip ranges through Colorado and Texas and well into Mexico. It is yellowish brown to dark brown, without the darker head and neck that are so characteristic of the eastern type. Sometimes there is a faint suggestion of cross-banding. The disposition and general habits of this snake are typically coach-whip, with its food running largely to lizards, other snakes, and desert rodents.

Another whip snake, found in the Rocky Mountain States and California, reddish brown in color, is generally known as the red racer. There are several distinct cross-bands on the neck, the first two or three quite dark, the rest fading abruptly towards the tail. Sometimes these bands run together, giving the snake a nearly black neck.

In the same regions, perhaps more commonly in the southern parts, one finds a similar snake that is black or blue-black in color. The underside may have a somewhat reddish or yellowish tinge, and there is a double row of dark patches towards the head. This is the so-called black whip snake which for many years has been considered a separate species. Recent investigation, however, has demonstrated that this serpent is merely a dark or melanistic phase of the red racer described above.

The striped whip snake is the smallest member of the group. Its maximum length is less than five feet. This slender snake, which is found from Oregon to Arizona, is brown on the back, but its sides are pale yellowish, each with five narrow brownish stripes. The lower surface is ivory-white, shading to pinkish toward the tail. Its habits are about the same as those of the other whip snakes.

The Pine Snake

The snakes of this genus are commonly divided into two groups, represented by the pine snake of the East in one, with the bull snake of the Middle West and the so-called gopher snake of the West Coast in the second. Each group is further divided into two or three races occupying various parts of its range.

The pine snake occurs from New Jersey to Florida, west as far as eastern Tennessee, and along the Gulf Coast to Alabama. In the northern areas it is a rather strikingly marked reptile with a back that is dull grayish white, grading to almost pure white on the sides. The back bears a series of deep black blotches, sharp and distinct on the lower portion of the snake but commonly running together and becoming less sharply outlined toward the head. Small dark blotches stand out vividly against the pale sides. Under-

YOUNG PINE SNAKE
Grayish white, with black markings. The adults are darker.

neath, the reptile is grayish white, more or less marbled with black. In the southern regions of the country, particularly in Florida, the pine snake is nearly uniform brown or grayish brown with the blotches only faintly discernible. The head is moderately small; the upper jaw protrudes over the lower one something after the fashion of a turtle. The scales are keeled, strongly on the back, and the tail terminates in a hard spine.

As its common name implies, this snake is met with most frequently in the pine barrens of our Atlantic coastal region. It is a strong and heavy serpent, averaging about five feet in length, with extra-large individuals stretching up to six and one half feet. A powerful constrictor, it chiefly feeds upon warm-blooded prey, such creatures as mice and rats, gophers and ground squirrels, small rabbits, and birds. During the nesting season the eggs of birds, especially ground-nesting varieties, form an important part of its diet. It has been recorded that the pine snake swallows an egg entire, and when it is part way down its gullet the reptile presses that portion of its body against the ground and then contracts powerful muscles to crush the shell. Most egg-eating snakes simply engulf the whole egg and then wait for their digestive juices to dissolve the shell. The late Dr. Ditmars [8] reported that a fully grown pine snake (in captivity) had no trouble in swallowing five or six ordinary hen eggs.

The majority of pine snakes are mean-tempered. Young specimens are generally quiet and docile, but as they grow up they soon become cross and irritable, ready and anxious to strike at anyone who comes near them. They are especially noted for their hissing ability, and probably no other American snake can hiss louder. This is made possible by a thin, flexible organ (the epiglottis) in the throat, which acts just as when one holds a card endwise and blows hard against it. If the card is permitted to vibrate a little, it produces a loud and deep hiss. All the snakes of this group (genus *Pituophis*) are equipped with this noise-making apparatus, and all are equally noted for their hissing. Even when striking they commonly emit a sort of coughing hiss at the same instant.

Like many other snakes, the pine snake appears to be fond of sunning itself, and specimens are likely to be discovered while basking happily in one of the sandy areas that dot the pine country. If there is an avenue of escape, the reptile will lose no time in getting away, but if its retreat is cut off, the pine snake is no slouch in defending itself. It will elevate the fore part of its body until the head is high in the air, face its enemy, take an enormous breath, and expel this air with a loud and prolonged hiss. The tail vibrates rapidly, making a rattling sound if the snake is in dry leaves or twigs.

Late in the spring this species lays from six to twelve rather large eggs. The youngsters are quite vividly marked; across the front of the face they have a dark, mask-like line, not unlike that of a raccoon. The pine snake should rate as one of our most beneficial reptiles, since it annually destroys vast numbers of harmful rodents.

THE BULL SNAKE

The bull snake is closely related to the pine snake of the East. It occupies the Great Plains area of our country, from Canada to Mexico and from Indiana to the Rocky Mountains, being perhaps most abundant in the state of Texas.

The bull snake is a sturdily built, strong, and agile serpent, one of the largest we have. The record length is seven feet eight inches (Bailey [2]), but somewhat less than five feet would be a fair average. The color is yellowish brown or deep orange brown, with a series of squarish, dark brown or black blotches on the back and a row of smaller blotches, usually of a paler shade, on each side. The underside is yellowish, more or less blotched with black, especially near the sides. The head is relatively small and somewhat pointed, indicating the snake's burrowing habits. The scales are moderately keeled on the back and smooth on the sides.

When first encountered and cornered the bull snake will put up a vigorous fight, hissing fiercely and striking savagely. In captivity, however, it calms down very quickly, and quite unlike the pine snake it generally becomes docile and good-natured in a remarkably short time. Its usual mild-mannered demeanor, plus its impressive size, have made the bull snake a prime favorite with showmen. Any traveling carnival or medicine show worthy of the name is almost sure to feature a so-called snake charmer whose principal actors are likely to be snakes of this species.

The bull snake is a powerful constrictor, feeding mainly upon small mammals. The Great Plains area is the home of a vast number of rodents—gophers, prairie dogs, ground squirrels, rats and mice, spermophiles, rabbits and such—and the bull snake with its efficient burrowing habits, seems particularly well equipped and strategically situated to cope with them. Probably no other American snake is more valuable to the agriculturist than this one. It follows its prey underground, often wiping out whole families. Feeding under seminatural conditions in captivity has revealed that the bull snake may enter a ground squirrel's burrow and catch one of the inmates, and while constricting it, if a second rodent at-

BULL SNAKE
Yellowish brown, with dark brown or black blotches.

tempts to rush past and escape, the snake will press the second ground squirrel against the side of the burrow with a portion of its body and hold it there until it completes killing the first one. Birds and birds' eggs are also eaten, and, in captivity at least, the bull snake will eat frogs.

Ranging as it does from Canada to Mexico, one cannot designate a common breeding month for this species. When the weather gets really warm it lays from ten to twenty eggs, each about the size of a small hen egg. They hatch in a few weeks, the youngsters measuring about fifteen inches in length.

The bull snake is not so dependable for a pet as some of the other large snakes, notably the mud snake and the king snake, but the majority of individuals are safe and easy to handle. They usually accept food readily and are generally hardy in captivity.

THE PACIFIC BULL SNAKE

This species is popularly known as the gopher snake in California because it eats, among other things, the pocket gophers that are so numerous there. It seems that the Pacific bull snake would be a better common name, since the name "gopher snake" is popularly applied to the indigo snake of the Southeast.

This species occurs from California north to British Columbia. It is a moderately large snake, averaging from four feet to nearly five feet in length, with occasional specimens topping the five-foot mark. It is rather slender for a bull snake, but quick in action and a strong constrictor. The ground color is pale yellowish brown, and there is a pattern of rather large, squarish blotches on the back. These are dark grayish brown or black in color. The lower surface is pale gray or white, with a row of small dark blotches near the sides. The scales are keeled.

This is a terrestrial snake, normally found in open country where it enjoys basking in the sun, although during hot weather it frequently resorts to swampy country or along the borders of streams. It even enters the water voluntarily and swims well when occasion demands.

The Pacific bull snake feeds chiefly upon warm-blooded prey, and it has the reputation of being one of the best mousers among our snakes. There is a record of thirty-five small mice taken from the stomach of one specimen (Pack [10]) of a related race. Gophers, rats, spermophiles, small rabbits, and birds are also eaten.

In spite of its fairly large size the Pacific bull snake is reported as being rather timid. Though a freshly caught specimen will defend itself in no uncertain manner, it is not so vicious as the other members of its group. Most individuals tame very quickly, are hardy in captivity, and accept food with little hesitation. Late in

July the Pacific bull snake lays from eight to about twenty eggs which hatch early in the fall, the young snakes being about one foot in length.

THE GREEN SNAKES

We have two species of green snake, commonly called grass snakes. They are both dainty and colorful and about as mild-mannered as any reptile could possibly be. Freshly caught specimens will submit to the roughest sort of treatment with the best of good nature. Perhaps the best known is the smooth green snake, so let us consider that one first.

As the popular name implies, this snake has smooth scales. It is not a large or even medium-sized snake, commonly measuring little more than one foot, but rarely attaining a length of two feet. Its color is a delicate pale green above, with no traces of spots or stripes, and greenish white below. With an individual that has just shed its skin, the green is extremely bright and vivid. The surface of the serpent has a satiny luster, something like the "finish" on a blacksnake.

In one or more of its subspecies the smooth green snake is to be found over a large portion of this country. Its favorite haunts are the lush meadows and grassy fields that are bordered by thickets. Here it finds an abundance of prey in the form of crickets, spiders, grasshoppers, and various grubs and caterpillars, for the snake is almost, if not completely, insectivorous. It is capable of climbing into the branches of thickets but spends the greater part of its time among the grass roots. It seems to know full well the value of its harmonizing color, and as a rule it moves very slowly and deliberately. When discovered it is more likely to "freeze" and trust to its protective coloration than it is to try for a quick get-away.

This snake presents a very good example of Nature's camouflage, for although it is far from rare it is not very often seen. The best time to find a specimen is late in the summer when insect life is most abundant. By carefully searching among the grasses and weeds near the edge of a moist meadow, you may be rewarded, although my own experience leads me to admit that most of the green snakes I have collected were the result of sheer accident.

Smooth green snakes are among the best of all species for pets. The tiny teeth are too small and weak to scratch the tenderest of skin, even if an individual had the notion to bite, and no green snake of the writer's acquaintance has ever entertained any such notion. They may be carried about in one's pocket without any

SMOOTH GREEN SNAKE
Pale leaf green.

attempt at escape. Their gentle disposition, plus their attractive color, make them ideal specimens to use when attempting to interest youngsters in snakes and their value to the farmer.

The other green snake, having keeled scales, is appropriately called the rough green snake. It is also known as the green whip snake and the magnolia snake. This is a rather long and slender snake, not much bigger around than the one just described, but attaining a length of close to two feet and a maximum length of slightly exceeding a yard.

This is chiefly a southern snake. Its upper surface is the same uniform, delicate, leaf green as that of the smooth green snake, but its lower surface is yellow. In some sections the ranges of the two species overlap, but there is no difficulty in distinguishing them by the color of their bellies and the character of their scales.

The rough green snake, which is a better climber than the smooth one, spends a large part of its time among the branches of bushes, vines, and low trees where its harmonizing shade matches the foliage so perfectly that the reptile is amazingly hard to see. It feeds upon insects, being very fond of the soft-bodied larvae of various night-flying moths. Like the other green snake, this one too is beneficial to the farmer and orchardist, ridding his plants and trees of a great many injurious insects during the year.

The rough green snake is just as good-natured as the smooth one and makes just as good a pet. Both species are so gentle that they may be handled with safety from the moment they are captured.

Both green snakes are egg-layers. The eggs are very elongate and few in number, usually numbering fewer than a dozen. They are deposited early in the summer, commonly under some flat stone at the edge of a grassy meadow.

The brilliant green of freshly shed specimens of either of these two snakes has prompted many a boy to try preserving an example or two in alcohol. Unfortunately, such preserved specimens soon fade to a weak, pale, bluish gray.

The Hog-Nosed Snake

This snake might be considered the clown of the serpent tribe in this country. If not the clown, then certainly the best actor. It is a stocky fellow, averaging about two feet in length, with the largest recorded specimen measuring forty and one-half inches (Ditmars [8]).

It has more common or popular names than any other American snake, and these names all suggest a very dangerous reptile indeed. But the snake itself is just about as dangerous as a rabbit! Some of the terrifying names applied to this species are sand viper, blowing viper, spreading adder, puff adder, and flat-headed adder, and a few other horrifying combinations of "adder" and "viper," even though there are no true vipers or adders in this country.

The hog-nosed snake occurs from New Hampshire to Florida and westward to the Rocky Mountains. It has a heavy, stubby body and a rather large head with a distinctly turned-up, swine-like snout. The snake is about as lithe and graceful as a length of sausage! The

HOG-NOSED SNAKE
Yellowish to orange-brown, with darker blotches.

general color is yellowish brown. On the back is an irregular pattern of squarish patches of dark brown or black. Smaller blotches on the sides alternate with those on the back. The lower surface is yellowish green, with splashes of black at the edges. The hog-nose is likely to be found in several different kinds of country, being equally at home in the deep woods, in sandy fields, in open swamps, or in the family garden. Specimens living in open, dry places are usually light sandy yellow, while those that live in moist, heavily-wooded areas are likely to be darker brown. Every so often we run across a pure black (melanistic) individual, with the pattern partially or completely obscured. The specimen in the accompanying illustration, photographed while putting on its "act," was rich olive green in color. The scales are rather prominently keeled.

The hog-nose is certainly not built for speed. It is extremely fond of sunning itself, and is commonly discovered happily coiled

HOG-NOSED SNAKE (BLACK PHASE)

in a plowed field or at the edge of an open, sandy road where there is little or no cover to hide in. The serpent is not poisonous in spite of what most country dwellers believe, and so, finding itself confronted with possible danger, and being unable either to fight or to run away with any degree of efficiency, the snake decides, with commendable wisdom, to put up a little bluff.

It makes no effort to escape when confronted by a potential enemy. Instead, it faces the intruder, raises its head a few inches off the ground, and spreads the upper portion of its neck until it is astonishingly thin. Some of the really dangerous cobras spread their so-called hoods in the same manner. The hog-nose hisses loudly, and at length, and if approached too closely, its mouth flies open and the snake makes short, threatening strikes at the object that is disturbing it. The serpent certainly has all the appearances

THE HOG-NOSED SNAKE PUTS ON ITS ACT

Upper left, on the alert. Upper right, threatening the enemy. Lower left, completely "dead." Lower right, the snake "recovers."

of a deadly reptile. Beside one, moreover, a really mad copperhead would appear almost angelic by comparison. In spite of all this fuss, though, the hog-nose is completely harmless. It could not be induced to bite, even if you were to put your finger in its mouth! The sole object of its hostile actions is to frighten you into leaving it alone. Even if the snake does strike, it will do so with its mouth closed, merely giving you a light thump! These antics are no doubt very successful against many of the snake's natural enemies, as it is easy to imagine a dog or fox hesitating to attack a creature that is apparently so well able to put up a defense, and deciding to look elsewhere for a more appetizing and less dangerous meal. As a matter of fact the respect with which the so-called "flat-headed adder" is regarded by most people suggests that the bluff is not altogether unsuccessful with the human race!

The second part of this snake's act is more interesting and far more unusual than the first part. If the reptile sees that you are not going to get frightened, it will apparently suffer a sudden con-

HEAD OF HOG-NOSED SNAKE   A THREATENING
                                  HOG-NOSED SNAKE

vulsion. The mouth gapes open and the serpent writhes and squirms in apparent agony, finally rolling over on its back. There it continues to thrash around until its mouth is coated with dirt, twigs, and leaf fragments. Then, with a final quiver of the tail, the snake seems to die. At this stage it can be picked up, tossed into the air, tied in a knot, or hung over a fence. The body remains limp and lifeless, with the dirt-filled jaws wide open and the tongue hanging out. There is no evidence of life. Mr. Hog-nose could not possibly look more like a dead snake.

In common with most bluffers, however, the snake gives itself away by carrying the bluff too far. Turn a possum-playing hog-nose right side up on the ground and it will flip over on its back as if the body contained a steel spring. It is very plain that to him an honestly dead snake should at all times be bottom-side up!

If the observer remains quiet near by, the bluffing snake will slowly raise its head after a short period and peer anxiously in all directions. If the danger appears to have departed, the snake will turn over and wriggle off as fast as its overstuffed body will permit. If you jump up and take after it, however, it will promptly roll over and become limp in "death" again! Even newly hatched youngsters will go through with the whole procedure, but it should be understood that these are the antics of freshly captured hog-nosed snakes. After a few days in captivity they apparently realize the futility of such goings on and act like any other well-behaved snake.

The hog-nose is not a rare snake but it is not seen so often as most of our other serpents. Probably its habit of lying low when approached, rather than attempting a quick dash for safety, accounts for this. The species does not ordinarily enter the water nor does it climb trees. Its chief food item is the toad, although frogs and insects are also sometimes eaten. A specimen in one of our zoological parks is reported to have eaten a garter snake. It does not feed upon warm-blooded prey.

It is well known that toads resist being swallowed by inflating their bodies when seized, sometimes getting nearly as globular as an apple. The hog-nose overcomes this trick very neatly, for it is provided with an extra lance-like tooth in the back of its mouth, and this punctures and deflates the luckless amphibian when partly swallowed.

The hog-nose snake is an egg-layer, depositing from ten to thirty eggs late in July. The young snakes are about six inches long. They are marked like their parents but are gray rather than yellowish brown.

This is one of the best of all snakes to keep for a pet. It is extremely hardy and will accept food, in the form of a toad or frog, on the very first day. It will flatten its head and hiss fiercely for the first few days, impressing your friends and acquaintances no end, but there is no danger of being bitten. After a short time the reptile will actually seem to show signs of enjoyment upon being handled.

Chapter 5

HARMLESS SNAKES OF WOODED AREAS

The Pilot Blacksnake

When discussing the common blacksnake with people who live in the country, if you mention the fact that the snake's length is no greater than about six feet, you are certain, every so often, to encounter a person who will dispute it. Lots of hunters, fishermen, hikers, campers, and others who get about outdoors will declare that they have seen or killed blacksnakes much longer than that, and they are telling the truth. The catch is that we have two kinds of "black" snakes, the so-called common blacksnake and the pilot or mountain blacksnake. The latter serpent is not even closely related to the former, belonging to a different genus altogether, but it is black, and the majority of people simply do not know that there are two kinds.

The pilot blacksnake is one of the largest snakes found in this country. Its average length is in the neighborhood of four or five feet, but seven- or eight-foot specimens are not uncommon. The record appears to be eight feet five inches (Conant & Bridges [5]). The largest specimen ever collected by the writer was seven feet nine inches long. The pilot blacksnake is a husky and powerful reptile, with a large and broad head and scales that are feebly keeled. The color is a rich glossy black. In fact the snake usually has the appearance of having been varnished, in contrast to the dull, satiny black of the common blacksnake. Some of the scales along the side are edged with white, and when the skin is distended they give the reptile a somewhat speckled appearance. The lower surface is gray and there is a prominent white patch on the chin and throat.

The pilot blacksnake occurs from Ontario to Florida and west-ward to Texas and Illinois. In the southern part of its range it is called the black chicken snake or chicken blacksnake. Old-timers used to believe that this snake acted as a sort of scout or pilot for the rattlesnake, warning it of danger and leading it to safety. Both the pilot and the rattler prefer rocky, mountainous country, and the two reptiles are sometimes seen together, especially in the spring when they are emerging from hibernation. When suddenly en-

PILOT BLACKSNAKE
Glossy black, with occasional flecks of white.

countered the chances are that the poisonous serpent would stand its ground while the faster blacksnake would immediately start going places. Thus the observer would naturally see the pilot first and then the rattler, and after several such experiences it is not strange that people got the notion that one snake acted as a "pilot" for the other.

Mountain blacksnake is a better name for this snake, as it does occur most abundantly in hilly, rocky, or mountainous territory, especially in timbered areas. This does not mean that you will find them in no other places, for they often get down into grassy meadows and swamplands, especially in the late summer. They sometimes get into farm buildings and chicken coops, particularly in the South, when on the prowl for eggs or rodents.

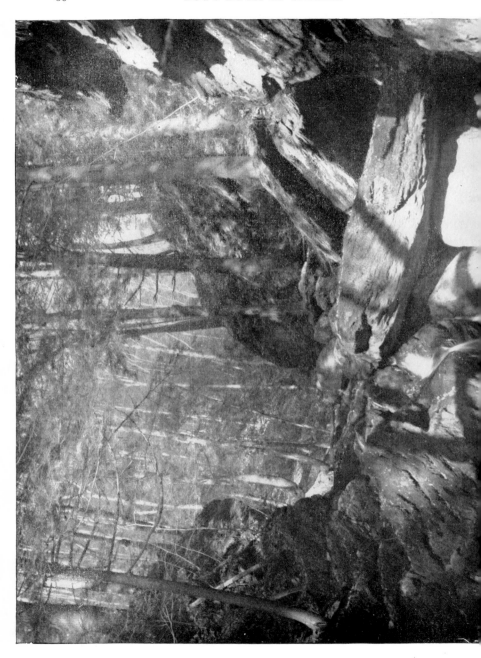

The pilot blacksnake, an excellent climber, frequently makes its home in a hollow tree. By gripping the rough bark with its belly-plates (scutes), it is able to climb even the perpendicular trunks of large trees with amazing efficiency. It is no uncommon sight to see a fine, sleek specimen stretched out on a horizontal limb several feet above the ground.

Unlike the common blacksnake the pilot is a true constrictor, killing rodents and birds by squeezing, but swallowing frogs alive like any nonconstricting snake. Large individuals are capable of engulfing small rabbits, and the snake's diet includes squirrels, rats and mice, birds and their eggs, frogs, lizards, and sometimes other snakes. It is nocturnal to a certain extent and during hot weather it chiefly hunts after dark.

The pilot blacksnake is a vicious fighter when first cornered, but it quiets down rather quickly and can generally be handled with reasonable safety after a few hours. After a week or so in confinement most pilot blacksnakes become very docile and seem to enjoy being handled.

Early in the summer this snake lays a dozen or so elongate white eggs, commonly in a hollow stump. They are quite large, about two inches long, and nearly an inch in diameter. Like those of the common blacksnake, the young of this reptile are gray, with brownish saddles on the back, so that from above they appear to be brown, ringed with gray. By the next fall they are shiny black like their parents. From the farmer's standpoint the pilot blacksnake is one of the most beneficial of snakes. It destroys creditable numbers of farm pests each summer.

THE RING-NECKED SNAKE

Sometimes when overturning stones or logs in the forest we uncover a small, dull, grayish black snake with a bright yellow collar around its neck. This is the ring-necked snake, a gentle little fellow found throughout most of this country.

The ring-neck averages about ten inches in length and it is seldom that one encounters a specimen over eighteen inches long.

The scales are smooth and the serpent has the same satiny luster that the common blacksnake has. The upper surface is a uniform deep slate-gray, and the lower surface is yellowish, verging on orange, usually with a row of black dots down the middle. Just back of the head is a narrow ring of yellow completely encircling

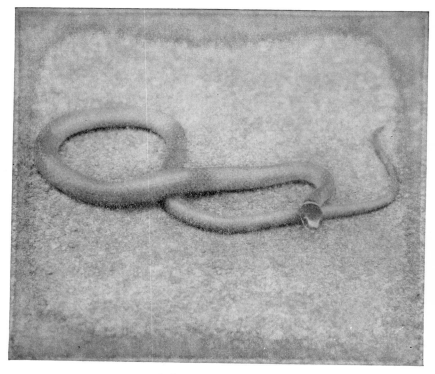

RING-NECKED SNAKE
Dull grayish black, with yellow collar. The underside is pinkish or yellowish.

the neck. Young specimens are usually a deeper black than adults, and the collars are more strongly portrayed, sometimes being more orange than yellow.

This small reptile is a lover of damp, woody areas, and besides being secretive and a good hider it is largely nocturnal in its habits. Consequently it is not observed so frequently as the garter snake or DeKay's snake. It is often considered to be quite rare in localities where it is really fairly abundant. Take a walk some morning down a woody ravine where there are several fallen trees, rotting stumps, and prostrate logs. On many of these old forest derelicts you will find large sections of the bark loose and capable of being pulled off in sizable pieces. Here is where you are likely to find specimens of the ring-necked snakes, sometimes four or five individuals under one piece, for the species is usually quite sociable in habits. Rolling over fallen logs and overturning flat stones among the moist leaves of the forest floor will probably turn out a few more. Yet you might stroll casually through those same woods every day for a whole summer without seeing a single ring-necked snake.

The food of this snake is about what one would expect it to be, considering the reptile's choice of hunting territory. Small snakes, earthworms, insect larvae, salamanders, small frogs such as "spring peepers," and partly grown wood frogs are on its bill of fare. Specimens have been known to devour small DeKay's and green snakes, but the ring-neck is not robust enough to cope with warm-blooded prey.

This is an egg-laying snake. The eggs are very thin-shelled and elongate, and their number is usually small. Hatching takes place much sooner than with most other snakes.

The ring-necked snake is entirely inoffensive and no amount of rough handling will induce it to show any signs of bad temper. It can hardly be rated a good pet, however, for if there is so much as a dead leaf in its cage the snake will crawl under it and keep out of sight most of the time.

THE WORM SNAKE

Once in a while we find what looks like a large and burly earthworm, but instead of a smooth, mucous-covered body, it is covered with tiny scales. This is the worm snake, a serpent that is far from rare, but one that is seldom observed owing to its retiring habits.

The worm snake occurs throughout most of this country from southern New England to the Gulf of Mexico and westward to

Nebraska and Texas. It averages some eight or nine inches in length, being just about the size of a robust "night crawler," and its wormlike appearance is further enhanced by the fact that it has no visible neck, the head grading into the body with no sign of a constriction where the neck should be. The color is dull grayish

WORM SNAKE
Pinkish brown, often iridescent.

brown on the back with the sides paler in tone; the underside is weak salmon pink. The scales are smooth and glossy, those along the sides somewhat opalescent. The head is small and rather bluntly pointed, and the eyes are very small. Young worm snakes are usually somewhat darker in hue than fully grown adults.

This species shows a preference for damp, wooded sections. It is semi-burrowing in its habits and will often be found under the moulding leaves that carpet the floor in hardwood forests. In searching for this diminutive reptile, flat stones and prostrate, moss-covered logs should be overturned in suitable locations, and the loose bark of rotting stumps and logs should be peeled off.

The worm snake's diet is composed almost entirely of earthworms. When in the wild state it will no doubt eat soft-bodied grubs and possibly small snails, but captive specimens generally refuse everything but earthworms.

About the first week in July the worm snake lays a small number of very elongate eggs, commonly about the roots of some decaying stump. A complete clutch is often only two or three eggs, and these hatch about the middle of September, the baby worm snakes, each about four inches long, immediately squirming down under the moist, decomposing leaves.

In the spring of the year and again in the fall worm snakes are occasionally turned up in moist fields where plowing is going on, but they are likely to be mistaken for earthworms unless one notices the active way in which the creatures attempt to burrow out of sight. Sometimes, after a prolonged rainy spell has saturated the ground for several inches, they will be found crawling on the surface, but as a general rule one needs to go poking under logs and into the forest debris in order to find this species. The worm snake is completely inoffensive and never has any thoughts about biting.

Like most burrowing snakes, however, it makes a discouraging pet, as it will keep out of sight practically all of the time.

A totally different kind of snake in the Southwest is sometimes known as a worm snake too. This is a small, brownish, blunt-headed little fellow, also bearing a superficial resemblance to a large earthworm.

These serpents are more correctly called "blind snakes," as the eyes are covered by the scales of the head, showing merely as dark spots. The animals are quite blind. True burrowing reptiles, they commonly live in anthills and look like polished worms. Comparatively little is known about the actual habits of the blind snakes. They are known to lay eggs, and they probably feed upon termites and other insects to a large extent.

The King Snake

The king snake group contains several kinds scattered over most of this country. They are mostly medium- to fair-sized serpents, cylindrical in shape, and are noted particularly for two things: their savage manners toward all other snakes, poisonous or non-poisonous, and their general good-natured demeanor toward man.

The so-called common king snake, or eastern king snake, is a strikingly marked fellow, averaging between three and four feet in length. The record appears to be five feet eight inches (Blanchard [4]). The color is glossy black, with narrow, white, equidistant rings that divide, or fork, on the sides and connect with one another to form a chainlike pattern. One of the reptile's popular names is chain snake. The lower surface is also black, more or less blotched with white. The common king snake ranges from New Jersey and southern Pennsylvania to northern Florida, and most of the specimens occurring in the northern part of this range are distinctly black and white. Farther south many individuals have yellowish markings in place of the white, and in the southern sections the ground color is brownish instead of black. Still farther south, in peninsular Florida, there are two subspecies of the common king snake, one pale greenish brown with indistinct cross-bands, and the other dull yellowish brown with no bands but with each scale tipped with dark brown, giving the snake a speckled appearance.

As a rule the king snake is an inhabitant of dry, wooded country, although individuals will be seen occasionally in marshy areas where they go in search of frogs. They have been observed entering the water voluntarily, and are good swimmers, but one usually associates the king snake with dry and forested regions. Not being good climbers, they spend most of their time on the ground, hiding under fallen logs during the daytime and doing most of their prowling after dark. They are not completely nocturnal, however, and are often seen abroad during the middle of the day.

The king snake is a constrictor; it feeds largely upon other snakes. These it first renders helpless by encircling them with several coils of its powerful body, and then begins by swallowing its victim headfirst. It does not hesitate to attack a snake larger than itself, and generally succeeds in distending its body sufficiently to engulf the larger reptile. It does not draw the line at venomous snakes, and commonly devours copperheads, moccasins, rattlesnakes, and even the deadly coral snakes. During the struggle the

KING SNAKE
Glossy black, with white markings.

king snake may be bitten repeatedly but it appears to be immune to venom. Since the poisonous snakes are not constrictors they have little chance against the steellike coils of the king snake.

The name "king snake" has been given to this serpent because it is such a successful fighter. It is the undoubted boss among our snake population, although the writer suspects that it would meet its match in a pine snake of comparable size. Many people regard it as the deadly enemy of the rattlesnake and therefore a friend of man. To the king snake, however, a rattlesnake, if not too large, is just another prospective meal, and if sufficiently hungry it will promptly move to the attack. It does not go out of its way to hunt for poisonous snakes, and by far the greater number of its victims are harmless varieties. The king snake also eats lizards and frogs, birds and small mammals, and eggs.

In spite of its fiercely aggressive attitude toward all other snakes, the king snake is surprisingly mild-mannered with man. Freshly captured specimens will resist by striking, but they calm down rather quickly and soon become remarkably tame and good-natured. Most individuals that have been kept for a few days may be handled with complete safety, and they even appear to enjoy being picked up. They are quite hardy in captivity. They accept food readily, in fact too readily sometimes, as many a snake fancier has discovered when he inadvertently placed a king snake and some other serpent in the same cage! This species, and the indigo snake, are perhaps the two best examples of the larger snakes (in the East) to be kept as pets.

The king snake deposits about a dozen eggs during the early summer, commonly among the roots of some decaying stump or under a mossy log. The young snakes appear in the late summer or early fall, and are just under one foot in length at the time of hatching.

Throughout much of its range the king snake is one of the few species that is commonly regarded as being beneficial. It is therefore afforded some measure of protection, or, more properly speaking, tolerance. As a matter of fact its economic value is questionable, for although it does kill an occasional venomous snake and a good many harmful rodents, the great majority of its victims are likely to be harmless snakes and lizards, many of which would destroy more mice and other crop pests in a season than the king snake would.

In the Mississippi Valley from Illinois to Louisiana, and from eastern Texas to Nebraska, the eastern king snake is replaced by a race known by several popular names, such as western king snake, Say's king snake, speckled or spotted king snake, and salt-and-pepper snake.

This reptile averages about three feet in length, with the largest individual recorded measuring five feet four inches long (Blanchard [4]). It is a rather husky serpent, greenish black in color, with each scale bearing a small pale green or white spot, so that the general appearance of the snake is decidedly speckled. Sometimes the spots tend to run together in places on the back to suggest narrow bands at regular intervals. The under side is whitish or yellowish, blotched rather heavily with black. The scales are smooth.

Like its eastern relative, this king snake shows a preference for shady locations and is most commonly found under a log or stone in some wooded ravine. It feeds upon various rodents, lizards and snakes, including the poisonous varieties, killing its prey by constriction.

This is another exceedingly mild-mannered reptile so far as man is concerned. It makes a splendid pet, seldom showing any signs of excitement or annoyance no matter how much it is handled. Its breeding habits are about the same as those of the eastern king snake, the average number of eggs being fewer than a dozen.

The yellow-bellied king snake is found in the Middle West from Indiana to Kansas, and south as far as Texas. About the same size as the western king snake just described, its colors and markings are quite different. The ground color is pale brown and on this is set a pattern of rather large, irregular, squarish blotches that are brownish or greenish in shade, each bordered by a narrow rim of black. The large blotches on the back alternate with smaller ones along the sides. The lower surface is yellowish, heavily splashed with black. The scales are smooth. As with several of our other snakes, the pattern is most striking on half-grown specimens. With old adults the ground color frequently becomes darkened, and the pattern consequently less distinct.

This king snake is more at home in open country than most of its group, and individuals are often found in open fields and pastures. It is also more of a daytime prowler than the majority of its relatives, and while it is occasionally seen abroad at night it does most of its hunting during the day. Like the other king snakes it will overpower and consume snakes and lizards, but its chief food appears to be rodents. Field and deer mice of several varieties that swarm over much of the prairie country inhabited by the yellow-bellied king snake make up the bulk of its prey.

This race of king snake is also very docile and well behaved in captivity, accepting food readily and permitting itself to be handled with no evidence of irritation.

Closely related to the last species is the brown king snake, popularly known as the mole snake. This is a reptile of the Southeast, occurring from Maryland to Florida, and ranging westward to Tennessee. It is a rather stocky snake, about three and one half feet long, with a relatively small head and practically no neck. As one would guess from its shape, and from its popular name, it is a burrowing species.

The color is dull brown with a series of rather indistinct blotches on the upper surface, irregular in form and wavy in outline and edged with a narrow border of black. The pattern is often obscure, and especially with old individuals the snake is likely to appear a uniform brown. Some specimens may even show dark lengthwise stripes. The scales are smooth.

Not very much is certainly known about the habits of this species. It is not often observed above ground, most of the specimens obtained being discovered while plowing or otherwise disturbing the soil. Occasional specimens are found under stones or logs. In captivity the brown king is docile but rather sluggish, lacking the alertness of the other king snakes. It probably feeds upon lizards and other snakes, as well as on salamanders, rodents, and moles.

The California king snake is found from southern Oregon to Lower California and eastward as far as western Utah and Arizona. It averages between three and four feet in length, and is a sturdily built serpent, like most of its group, and a strong constrictor.

This snake is especially noted for the fact that it has two distinctly different color phases. The majority of specimens are coal-black, rich, and glossy, with a series of narrow white rings encircling the body. The other, and less common phase, is black, with a narrow white stripe running *lengthwise* down the middle of the back from just back of the head to the very tip of the tail.

For many years these were very naturally considered to be two entirely different snakes, and it was not until an able herpetologist (Klauber[9]) hatched some eggs from mothers of both color phases and succeeded in getting both kinds of young in the same litter that the surprising fact of dual pattern was established. The striped examples occur in the southern part of the species' range.

The California king snake feeds largely upon other snakes and is known to eat birds and small mammals. It becomes quite tame in captivity, and, like the others of its genus, can usually be handled without any fear of being bitten.

The scarlet king snake is a brilliantly colored fellow, making up in gaudy hues what it lacks in size. It is the smallest of the king snakes, averaging about eighteen inches in length and apparently never exceeding two feet. It is rather slender for a king snake, but a strong constrictor nonetheless. Ounce for ounce or inch for inch it is just as good a battler as its larger relatives. It may be found from Delaware to Florida.

This snake is strikingly banded with red, yellow, and black. The flaming scarlet bands are widest, and in the majority of specimens they completely encircle the body. In the northern sections of the serpent's range the red bands commonly do not cross the underside. The yellow and black rings are much narrower. The serpent has a yellow collar, some black at the back of the head, and a red snout.

Scarlet king snakes are sometimes called "false coral snakes," owing to their close resemblance to that deadly species. In the coral snakes, however, the snout is always coal-black, and the arrangement of the color sequence is different. With the poisonous snake the red and yellow are in contact, while with the so-called "mimics" a ring of black always separates the red and yellow bands. This holds true for all the snakes in our country. This is not the case, however, in tropical South and Central America where there are several varieties of coral snakes with various color patterns.

The scarlet king snake is found most commonly under loose bark or fallen logs in shady, well-watered, timbered regions. It feeds upon salamanders, lizards, and small snakes, killing its prey by constriction as do the larger king snakes. Fledgling birds and small mice are also eaten. Insects and even small fish have been reported from the stomachs of these snakes.

In spite of its pugnacious attitude toward other snakes, the scarlet king snake is usually very good-natured with people. Most captive

SCARLET KING SNAKE   SCARLET SNAKE

Red, yellow, and black rings. The   Red, yellow, and black bands. The un-
snout is red.   derside is yellowish. The snout is red.

specimens appear to enjoy being handled and never display any evidence of temper. Like the other king snakes, this one lays eggs. The newly hatched youngsters have whitish rings in place of the yellow.

THE SCARLET SNAKE

The scarlet snake is another small, brightly colored reptile, easily mistaken for the scarlet king snake just described or for the coral snake. It, too, is often called a "mimic" of the latter serpent and is known as a "false coral snake."

The scarlet snake is a slender species, averaging about fifteen inches in length. The record is twenty-five inches (Ditmars [8]). It bears the same three colors, red, yellow, and black, but one might say that this snake is red with a series of black bands, each enclosing a yellow ring. In other words, the red bands predominate, while the black is merely a border to the smaller yellow bands. As with the other "mimics," the red and yellow do not come in contact. From above, the snake appears to be ringed with these three colors, but the bands stop at the underside, which is yellowish or pinkish white in marked contrast to the lower surface of the scarlet king snake. This species also has a red snout.

The scarlet snake is found from New Jersey to Florida, and westward in the South, as far as Oklahoma. It is rather closely related to the king snakes and is a powerful constrictor for its size. It is secretive in its habits, seeming to prefer damp, wooded areas. It is most often found under logs or burrowing about under the accumulation of decaying leaves on the forest floor. Observers have reported that when crawling on a firm surface the scarlet snake frequently carries its head and neck well off the ground, like a racer. Many of the king snakes have this same trait.

The food of the scarlet snake in the wild state is not very well known. Presumably it feeds on salamanders, lizards, small snakes, mice, and similar items. Captive specimens will accept baby mice and small snakes. This is also an egg-laying serpent, depositing a small number of eggs, six to nine, commonly under a rotting stump, late in June or early in July.

THE GROUND SNAKE

There are several varieties of closely related, small brown snakes, mostly living in the southern states and generally called brown snakes, ground snakes, or wood snakes. A good example would be the little fellow that occurs from New Jersey to Georgia and westward to southern Ohio and northern Alabama. This species is locally called the ground snake or wood snake.

It is a small variety, seldom exceeding ten inches in length. The color is chestnut brown above and yellowish white below, and there may be a double row of small black dots on the back. The body is rather stout in proportion to its length, the head is small and pointed, and the tail is short and rather abruptly tapering. The scales are smooth. This description appears quite like that of DeKay's snake, but the two reptiles are easily distinguished when seen together. This snake is stouter and stockier and it lacks the strongly keeled scales of DeKay's snake.

The ground snake is a secretive species, living for the most part in heavily timbered regions. It loves the moist, forested floor of some shady ravine where it prowls among the decaying leaves and rotting stumps and logs in search of worms and grubs. The snake is not very often seen, although it is far from rare. This is probably due to its small size, inconspicuous color, and the fact that it is more than likely to spend most of the day hiding under loose bark.

The ground snake is a gentle and inoffensive reptile, never showing any inclination to bite. It is about as safe to handle as the green snakes previously discussed. It does well in captivity, feeding willingly upon earthworms, but it does not make a very good exhibition specimen for it will insist on keeping out of sight if there is anything in its cage large enough to crawl under.

Chapter 6

HARMLESS SNAKES OF PONDS AND MARSHES

The Ribbon Snake

Near the writer's home is a perfect jewel of a tiny woodland pond. The brook, scarcely more than a yard in width, meanders lazily down through a tract of cut-over pasture land and enters an area of second-growth oak and hickory where there is a liberal sprinkling of birch trees. Here it encounters a small granite ledge, and before finding a way around this stony obstacle it backs up enough water to form a miniature lake just about the size of a tennis court. Rank grass grows in tussocks all around the edges, as well as out in the pond itself, for nowhere is the water more than a foot or so deep. Hardly large enough to interest a self-respecting water snake, this is Paradise Preferred to the ribbon snakes, and on nearly any sunny day two or three examples of this slender, vividly marked serpent may be seen lying motionless on some of the floating debris.

The ribbon snake does most of its hunting among the wet and tangled grassy borders of such diminutive ponds, but it enters the water readily and swims expertly, generally keeping to the surface with its head above water. When frightened, however, it can submerge and travel under water with the ease of a water snake.

The ribbon snake looks very much like our common garter snake, and it is safe to say that most of those observed are mistaken for the latter reptile. It is a remarkably slender snake, much more slender than the garter snake. The ground color varies from gray to greenish black, and when the light strikes it at certain angles it appears to be a rich brownish red. Like the garter snake it has three stripes running lengthwise down its body, one on the back and one on each side. These stripes are bright yellow, usually more

vivid than the garter snake's stripes. The lower surface is pale yellow, in contrast to the greenish white abdomen of the garter snake. The head is quite small with a narrow, vertical yellow mark in front of each eye. The scales are strongly keeled. The maximum length is about thirty-three inches, but any individual more

RIBBON SNAKE
Greenish black to rich brown, with vivid yellow stripes.

than two feet long can be considered a big one. The average specimen is about eighteen inches in length.

The ribbon snake is at most times a nervous, excitable reptile. A captured garter snake, after a brief period of resistance, will usually calm down and accept the situation with good grace, but not so the ribbon snake. This species seldom becomes docile no matter how much it is handled. Of course the slender snake is too small to do any harm; in fact, its teeth are so tiny that even though the creature strikes repeatedly, and most specimens will, it is rare that it succeeds in even scratching one's skin.

The food of this snake is just about what you would expect of a snake that haunts pond borders. Small frogs and tadpoles make up the bulk of its prey, with an occasional grub or earthworm on the side.

Ribbon snakes, in one of their races, may be found from Maine to Florida and westward to the Great Plains.

The Common Water Snake

The common water snake is familiar to all boys who have fre- quented the "old swimmin' hole" or fished in the old millpond. It is a heavy-bodied snake, a characteristic of many serpents that spend a large part of their life in the water. On bright days in midsummer we see them enjoying the sun's warmth as they bask on stones or stumps at the water's edge. Sometimes they climb up into the low bushes where they stretch out among the overhanging branches. They are seldom very far from the water that spells safety, however, and when danger threatens they slip quietly into the friendly water and hide from view. If a specimen is suddenly alarmed, it will fling itself into the pond with a great splash and thrash wildly for a second or two before diving for deep water.

As a rule the water snake, unless unduly alarmed, swims out a few feet and then comes to the surface with just its head above water. If the danger seems real, it then submerges with scarcely a ripple and hides among the rocks and weeds in rather deep water where it is able to remain for a surprisingly long time without com- ing up for air.

The water snake's chunky appearance and broad, flat head, to- gether with its aquatic environment, lead many folks to call it a "moccasin" and to regard it as deadly poisonous. The water snake is not poisonous, and is quite different from the chunky, white- mouthed true moccasins of our southern swamps. At the same time the common water snake is not a reptile to be fooled with, as most individuals have a vicious temper and strike repeatedly when cornered. While their bite carries with it no venom, the snake does possess long and sharp recurved teeth, and these are capable of inflicting a rather deep wound. Sometimes a specimen in captivity becomes docile and apparently good-natured, but what looks like

COMMON WATER SNAKE
Reddish brown, with brick-colored wavy bands. Old adults are a dingy brown.

good nature is more often mere sluggishness. As a rule a water snake should not be trusted very far.

The adult water snake is a rather ugly looking customer. The head is large and broad and the body is thick and heavy. The scales are strongly keeled. Young specimens, up to a foot and a half or so in length, are more graceful in appearance. The largest individual recorded measured four feet three inches (Conant [5] and Bridges), but the average length for a fully mature specimen is about thirty inches.

Young and partly grown water snakes are quite strikingly marked. The general shade is pale to rich brownish, with a slight tinge of reddish. On this ground color is laid a pattern of irregular, brown, wavy cross-bands. These bands are broadest on the back, narrowing somewhat on the sides, and toward the tail they tend to break up into blotches. The underside is mottled with gray and black and sometimes with red. On an individual that has just shed its skin the colors are vivid and sharply defined. Old specimens generally lose their bands or have them only faintly discernible. They become an almost uniform dingy brown in color.

The water snake feeds chiefly upon fish and frogs. Examinations of stomach contents show that these two items make up about 80 per cent of their food, with a fair amount of salamanders and tadpoles, a few insects, and, very rarely, a mouse or shrew. Trout fishermen frequently condemn this snake in no uncertain terms, claiming that it destroys large numbers of game fish. But even though the water snake is an able swimmer it seems probable that the slower-moving, nongame fishes, such as the dace and suckers, make up the bulk of their catch. Aquatic insects are also eaten, and since many of the latter feed voraciously upon trout spawn, perhaps the water snake is in truth more beneficial than harmful to the sportsman's interest. There is no doubt, however, about the reptile's being a most serious pest around fish hatcheries and also along small streams during dry seasons when the trout are hampered in their movements. Water snakes have to be eliminated or rigidly controlled in such places.

Living as it does in a watery environment, many people believe that the water snake must take a heavy toll from birds that habitually choose wet locations for their nesting sites. Such birds as the red-wing blackbird, swamp sparrow, and various ducks must offer tempting tidbits during the season of eggs and nestlings, but there is little evidence to support the belief. The water snake appears to be completely satisfied with a steady diet of cold-blooded animals.

Water snakes give birth to living young and generally have rather large families. They are born late in the summer, usually in August or September. The average number is about thirty, but a female in the possession of the writer had a brood of forty-four. Each was about eight inches long and was quite colorful, with distinct brown saddles on a pale gray ground color. They bore little resemblance to their ugly maternal parent.

The common water snake is found throughout most of the northeast part of the country, southward to the vicinity of southern Tennessee, and westward to Kansas and Oklahoma. The southern banded water snake is a variety much like the common one, but its bands extend the full length of the body and its underside is yellowish, heavily spotted with black and red. Its habits and dispositions are about the same as those of the snake just described; it is a very common serpent in the swamps and rivers of the southeastern United States. Another variety, the flat-tailed water snake, lives in the coastal regions of Florida. This differs from all other American snakes in having the last few inches of its tail compressed vertically, like the true sea snakes, but to a lesser degree. This snake, only a couple of feet long, prefers to live in the brackish water of mangrove swamps. One or two other subspecies of the common water snake, differing slightly from the eastern variety, are found in the Mississippi Valley. There are no members of this group in our western states.

THE RED-BELLIED WATER SNAKE

The red-bellied water snake, known throughout its range as the "copper belly," is a rather large and stout reptile that is found from northern Virginia to South Carolina and westward as far as eastern Oklahoma. Its maximum length is about four and one half feet, with the average specimen measuring a little more than one yard. In this species the bands are absent or very poorly defined, and the serpent's back appears to be a uniform dark brown or greenish black. The underside is solid brick-red. Juvenile specimens are marked with brownish blotches on a lighter ground color, but as they mature they put on the uniform color of the adults. Even with the youngsters, however, the lower surface is an immaculate red.

This snake has about the same habits and lives in the same kind of territory as the banded water snake. Its favorite home is in the quiet cove of some small, weed-grown pond, where it loves to climb out on stumps or stones on which it can bask in the sun. It is a rather timid snake, or perhaps we should say a wise one, for it has learned to plunge into the water and take refuge among the aquatic vegetation at the first sign of approaching danger. When cornered, however, there is nothing timid about the way this fellow defends itself, for it will strike savagely until overpowered.

Its food consists of various cold-blooded animals that are to be found in the same environment. Fish, frogs, tadpoles, newts, salamanders, and crayfish are recorded on its bill of fare. Like most of the other water snakes this one is hardy in captivity, generally takes food readily, and appears to accept confinement with good grace. After a few weeks in captivity specimens are less apt to strike than are many of the other members of the water snake group, but it pays to be cautious when handling large specimens of this serpent.

The red-bellied water snake gives birth to living young, usually in the late summer. The average number is about twenty. The youngsters are about nine inches long and are rather boldly banded at birth.

This snake is not found in New England or in our other more northern states. "Red-bellied" water snakes from these regions usually turn out to be common water snakes, which themselves sometimes have considerable amounts of red on their underside.

THE GREEN WATER SNAKE

Living in the larger swamps, sluggish creeks, and quiet ponds of the South we find a water snake that might well claim the championship in size for all United States snakes, so far as circumference is concerned. It is not so very long, the largest specimen recorded being five feet in length (Conant [5] and Bridges). Its average length is only a little more than a yard, but with an old individual the girth is out of all proportion to the reptile's length.

This is the green water snake, at home in the coastal marshes of South Carolina and Georgia, throughout Florida and the Gulf States, and up the Mississippi Valley as far as southern Illinois. The color above is dark greenish brown or greenish gray, with a series of narrow blackish cross-bands that are usually weakly defined. As with many of the other water snakes, the pattern tends to fade

GREEN WATER SNAKE

Greenish gray, with weak bands of black. Old specimens are a dull greenish brown.

with age. Large specimens are commonly a uniform dull greenish gray. The lower side is pale yellow for most of its length, with the rear portion grayish brown flecked with black and yellow. The head is very large and broad and the scales are strongly keeled.

Despite its overstuffed, clumsy appearance, the green water snake is a good climber that enjoys sunning itself among the forks of trees which overhang a pond. The reptile probably rarely leaves its watery home except for these arboreal excursions, for on dry land a really big individual is at a distinct disadvantage. There it is only by a supreme effort that it can hunch its heavy body along, but in the water the snake is well able to take care of itself. It dives and swims expertly, showing surprising speed and grace when necessary. Like most of our other water snakes, this one feeds mainly upon fish and frogs. It does a considerable part of its prowling at night.

The young are born alive, generally in rather small broods. From ten to fifteen appears to be the average. As a rule the young snakes are born in late July or August. They usually average about ten inches in length.

This is a very hardy snake in captivity, generally accepting food readily. It is, however, a sluggish reptile that usually spends most of its time asleep in a corner of its cage. It is not so vicious in disposition as many of the other water snakes, and some specimens become fairly tame after a short period of confinement. At the same time, however, it pays to exercise the utmost caution when handling a specimen, for it can strike with speed and precision in spite of its pudgy appearance. The large head is armed with sharp, curving teeth that can produce a slashing wound.

The Brown Water Snake

The brown water snake is nearly as fat as the species just described, and it tops the green water snake in length. Its average is about three and one half feet, but the snake is reported to attain a maximum length of close to six feet in exceptional cases. It is generally considered to be our largest water snake.

This is the "water pilot" or "water rattle," generally feared throughout its range and believed by many to be deadly poisonous. It is, of course, nonpoisonous, but it is a very rugged and sturdy serpent, large of head and stout of body. It looks dangerous enough to fool almost anyone. It is common in most of the lakes, rivers, ponds, and creeks of the Gulf States, eastward to Florida and northward to the Carolinas.

The general color is rusty brown, with a series of darker brown patches in the form of squarish marks on the back. Old specimens are usually dull brown with but slight traces of the marks. The underside is yellowish, blotched and speckled with black. The head is long, swollen at the temples, and the neck is relatively small, thus proving as false the old saying that you can tell a venomous snake by its large, triangular head. The scales are heavily keeled.

Besides being our largest water snake this fellow would also undoubtedly win first prize for being the most ugly both in looks and in disposition. The snake is rather timid and shy in the wild state, and tries its level best to keep well out of man's way. When cornered, however, it fights savagely and seldom develops anything like tameness. Since they rarely accept food in captivity, the majority of captive water pilots remain sullen and vicious until they starve to death.

Fish seem to make up the bulk of this snake's diet, with frogs and toads, small turtles, and salamanders on the side. It is not believed that it eats warm-blooded prey. Perhaps no other water snake is as fond of sunning itself as is this one. It is a rather social creature, and frequently several individuals are to be seen sharing the same log or stump for their sun bath. Since these snakes are excellent climbers, many of the bushes that border the water have clusters of them entwined about their sturdier branches on sunny days. The water pilot is said to commonly wind the end of its tail about some aquatic plant, thereby providing itself with a serviceable anchor, and then float upright in the water with its head just at the surface.

Like the other water snakes, this one gives birth to living young, usually in August. The broods are rather large as a rule, and the newly born snakelets are usually about twelve inches long.

The Queen Snake

Out in the central part of the country, in the vicinity of Ohio and Indiana, we find a rather slender water snake known as the queen snake. It does not live west of the Mississippi River, and its eastern limit appears to be in the neighborhood of western Pennsylvania.

This is not a large serpent, the average length being about twenty inches. The color is brown, generally rich and dark. As a rule there are three darker stripes running the length of the back, but these may be rather indistinct or even lacking. There is also a longitudinal stripe of yellow well down on each side, while the underside is pale yellow with a pair of brownish stripes down the middle. Most of our water snakes are marked with bands that run across the body, but in this much striped serpent they all run lengthwise. The scales are keeled.

The queen snake is supposedly a lover of clean, fresh, running water, and is most frequently seen along small streams, hilly brooks, and similar clear, fast-moving watercourses. At the same time the snake is not rare in canals and other quiet bodies of water. Unlike the other water snakes, which eat quite a variety of aquatic food, this fellow feeds almost exclusively upon one item, the crayfish. It is known to eat fish sometimes, and probably would not refuse a frog or a tadpole when really hungry, but observations by competent herpetologists clearly indicate that the queen snake prefers crawdads above all other things.

Like the other water snakes, this one is fond of basking in the sun, a favorite place being some flat stone at the water's edge. The reptile, which is a very capable climber, commonly coils among the branches of low shrubs that overhang the stream.

The queen snake is remarkably docile for a water snake, and while a freshly caught specimen may attempt to defend itself by biting, it seldom takes very long for it to calm down and become well behaved. It does not take well to confinement, as a rule, most individuals refusing to eat. Snake specialists report that it is difficult to keep this species contented and in good health for any length of time. The young snakes are born alive, and the broods are usually few in number.

The Mud Snake and the Rainbow Snake

These are two better than fair-sized snakes found in our southern swamplands that are popularly believed, by some of the natives, to be "hoop snakes" and therefore very dangerous. You will remember from Chapter 2 (page 16) that the hoop snake was supposed to have a deadly sting in its tail. Both of these snakes have small, horny spines at the end of the tail, and these spines are rigid enough to prick the skin. Sometimes one of these snakes, in a frantic effort to escape, may wind its tail around a person's wrist or arm and the tail tip may scratch the skin a little but there is no venom involved. Both these snakes are entirely harmless. These

RED-BELLIED MUD SNAKE
Glossy deep purplish black, with red markings along the sides.

two are the mud snake and the rainbow snake. Let us consider the mud snake first.

This is a rather sluggish, good-natured serpent that could well be classified as large both in length and circumference. The average length is about four feet, with the largest specimen recorded measuring five feet nine inches (Smith [11]). The upper surface is deep purplish black with a series of inverted red V-shaped marks on the sides. The scales are smooth, large, and glossy, and they impart a shiny, varnished appearance to the reptile.

This species is known by a number of popular names. Red-bellied mud snake, horn snake, stinging snake, hoop snake, and stingaree are a few examples. It is a burrowing snake whose favorite home is in the timbered swamplands of the South. Here it lurks under fallen logs and rotting stumps or burrows about in the oozy mud and digs deep into the soft clay banks of creeks. Individuals have been collected from several feet underground. Little was known about this snake's feeding habits until a few years ago. Specimens that were brought north for exhibition in zoological parks invariably starved to death after a few months, absolutely refusing to accept fishes, frogs, tadpoles, and similar food that one would ordinarily expect a swamp-dwelling reptile to eat.

Experiments in Louisiana by Mr. G. P. Meade established that the mud snake will eagerly devour the tailed amphibian popularly known as the congo eel, while showing little or no interest in other denizens of the marshes. It is probable that the mud snake eats some of the other salamanders in a wild state, but now that its favorite food is known it is no longer a puzzle to keep this burly and showy serpent in good shape for exhibition.

The mud snake is a sluggish and mild-mannered fellow that does not in the least resent handling. A freshly caught specimen will struggle somewhat in an effort to get away, and it may succeed in giving its captor a slight jab with its tail spine. The snake never seems to consider trying to bite, however, and after it has been held captive for a brief time it may be picked up without any qualms. Being both husky and colorful it makes an excellent snake for demonstration purposes as it may be passed from hand to hand with complete confidence.

The mud snake is an egg-layer, depositing from twenty to forty elongate white eggs in the summer. The female probably remains with her eggs until they hatch. Mr. Meade found his captive specimens coiled about the eggs in one corner of the cage, and although they left their eggs several times in the next few weeks, either to shed their skins or to eat, they always returned and coiled about them again. Other observers have reported finding this species coiled about a clutch of eggs in the wild state, usually beneath a log or plank. The purpose of this maternal care is probably to protect the eggs from prowling predators rather than to incubate them.

The rainbow snake is very much like the mud snake, except for color. The general ground color is purplish black or deep blue, and there are three longitudinal stripes of dark red or orange extending from just back of the head to the tail. A broad stripe of pale yellow is present on each side, and the underside is pinkish with dark blotches. The rainbow snake is certainly well named, being one of the most colorful of our serpents. The scales are smooth, and the whole animal has a glossy, polished appearance. Its average length is about four feet, with the largest specimens not much over five.

The rainbow snake, like the mud snake, prefers to live in heavily timbered swamps, and the few specimens that are found are usually discovered under prostrate logs. They burrow into the clay banks of creeks, and Cope [6] reported digging a specimen from a clay bank beneath ten feet of sand. Individuals have been taken in sandy fields, which illustrates the fact that it is risky to relegate any snake to a certain type of environment.

Again like the mud snake, this species is exceptionally gentle and does not resent handling. A freshly caught specimen will thrash from side to side like a fish held out of the water. Though the reptile may prod you a little with its horney tail spine, there is no danger of being bitten.

Little is known regarding the habits of this snake, and there is an opportunity here for some energetic southern youngster to add to our knowledge about American snakes. It probably feeds on fish and frogs, or like the mud snake mostly upon a single species of salamander. Captive specimens almost always refuse to eat and ultimately starve to death. This is indeed most unfortunate, as such a handsome snake should be a part of every reptile exhibition.

The rainbow snake's choice of a home in almost inaccessible swamp country, plus its apparent scarcity, means that relatively few individuals are ever encountered. Once a specimen has been seen, however, it will not be forgotten. Its range is from southern Maryland to Florida and Alabama.

The rainbow snake is also an egg-layer, generally depositing from twenty to forty eggs in the latter part of the summer. The young snakes are about nine inches long when hatched.

THE FOX SNAKE

Like many another harmless snake, the fox snake possesses scent glands near the base of its tail. When irritated it discharges a fluid which, in the case of this particular reptile, is said to have somewhat the same odor as that often present in cages containing foxes. Baird [3] and Girard, back in 1853, noted the similarity and named this species *vulpina,* which is Latin for "foxlike."

The fox snake is well known in the Middle West, being at home from eastern Ohio to Nebraska. It is a fairly large snake, averaging between three and four feet in length, with the largest specimen recorded measuring five feet five inches (Conant [5]). It is a rather stoutly proportioned serpent, with the tail tapering somewhat abruptly to a sharp point. The ground color is pale brown or yellowish tan, and on this is laid a pattern of deep brown or black more or less conspicuous blotches extending all the way down the back. Smaller and less conspicuous blotches are present on each side. The head is reddish brown, sometimes almost coppery, and the snake's underside is yellow liberally speckled with black. The scales are keeled.

The fox snake is frequently mistaken for one of our venomous snakes, for its bold, blotchy appearance and rather stout form is faintly suggestive of the timber rattlesnake, while the reddish tinge on its head makes one think of the copperhead. Various popular names for this snake include redhead, pine snake, and spotted adder.

In the western portions of its range this snake is found in a variety of different places such as prairie, farmlands and fields, swampy country, and even in deep woods. In the east the fox snake is nearly always to be found in wet, marshy territory or in fields immediately adjacent. An excellent swimmer, it has been observed more than a mile from shore in some of the large midwestern lakes. A very common place to find a specimen on a warm sunny day is on the top of a muskrat house, where the reptile coils contentedly in the sun.

The fox snake is a poor climber and seldom gets very far above the ground, but it will climb into low bushes and shrubs to get at birds' eggs. It feeds largely upon warm-blooded prey which it kills by constriction. Probably its greatest source of food is the ever-present supply of meadow mice, the rodents that generally live in large numbers in the same sort of marshy country that the fox snake selects for a home. Rats and small mammals such as rabbits are known to be eaten, and specimens of the reptile living in wooded areas undoubtedly consume deer mice and squirrels. Birds' eggs and fledglings are an accepted part of its diet, and it is easy to conceive of the fox snake's threading its way among the reeds and rank grasses in the early summer and chancing upon many a song sparrow's, bobolink's, or blackbird's nest.

The fox snake is an able fighter when cornered. Most specimens resist capture in no uncertain manner, striking viciously and hissing loudly in a sharp, sneezing sort of way. The snake usually gets over its show of bad temper in a fairly short time, and the majority of individuals become docile and well behaved within a few days, permitting handling with little evidence of annoyance. The fox snake is hardy in captivity, usually accepts food readily, and is one of the best of our larger snakes for exhibition purposes.

Sometime after mid-July the fox snake lays from ten to twenty elongate eggs. These have a granular surface and commonly adhere together. The baby fox snakes, which average about ten inches in length, are very brightly marked.

The fox snake's preponderant diet of rodents makes it one of the most beneficial of serpents. It would be to the best interest of every farmer and orchardist if this species could be given the protection it deserves.

Chapter 7

POISONOUS SNAKES OF THE UNITED STATES

The reason most people fear snakes and have such a deep-rooted dread of encountering one is that we have among our snake population a few that are really dangerous. The harmless varieties outnumber the poisonous ones by a large margin, and here in this country a person may spend a lifetime in the fields and woodlands of his neighborhood without ever seeing a venomous snake. The few bad actors, however, have to be reckoned with, and every boy or girl who goes hunting or fishing, camping or berrypicking, or for any other reason hikes out into the country, should learn to recognize these dangerous serpents and distinguish them from the harmless kinds. In this way they will save themselves many anxious moments of needless apprehension. If there is ever any uncertainty about a reptile's identification, however, always give the snake the benefit of the doubt and treat *all* snakes with caution until you are absolutely sure of what you are dealing with.

The poisonous snakes of the world are divided into four principal groups: the cobra group, the vipers, the pit vipers, and the sea snakes, which are allied to the cobra group. We have in this country two species (plus two varieties) of coral snakes, which belong to the cobra group, and several species of the pit viper group. There are no true vipers here, and the sea snakes probably never reach our shores, although one variety occasionally gets as far north as Lower California on the Mexican Pacific Coast.

The copperhead, the water moccasin, and all of the rattlesnakes are pit vipers, so called because of a deep pit on each side of the head between the nostrils and the eyes. This feature, which is quite noticeable, serves as a sensory organ and is not present in the true vipers. The eyes of our pit vipers have vertical pupils, like those of a cat during the daytime, and it is often stated that you can tell a poisonous snake by its eyes. It is true that our harmless snakes, with the exception of the boas and about half a dozen others, all have round pupils, so the rule holds true fairly well in this country, although the deadly coral snakes of our southern states have round pupils too. Several nonpoisonous foreign snakes, such as the py-

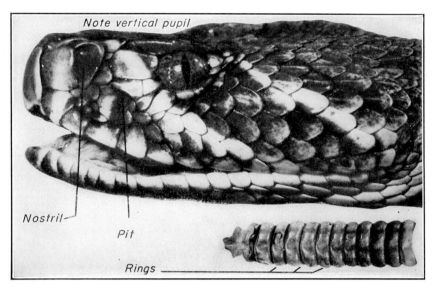

Note vertical pupil

Nostril

Pit

Rings

HEAD AND RATTLE OF THE DIAMOND-BACK RATTLESNAKE—
A TYPICAL PIT VIPER

thons, have vertical pupils, and some really dangerous snakes of other lands have round ones.

The poison apparatus of the pit vipers consists of two long and hollow teeth, one on each side, rigidly fastened to each upper jaw. When the snake's mouth flies open, these teeth (fangs) spring into position. There is a sheaf of thin flesh covering the fangs, and this is withdrawn when the reptile strikes. The venom is contained in a pair of modified salivary glands situated behind the eyes. When the snake strikes its victim, venom is forced through the hollow fangs and into the wound by way of tiny openings near their tips, on the principle of a pair of hypodermic needles. The strike of one of these snakes usually leaves two small punctures, while bites of nonpoisonous snakes generally leave a curving row of tooth marks or a series of scratches.

The fangs are not permanent structures but are shed at intervals. New ones are constantly forming in the upper jaws, and by the time one is ready to be lost (it is generally left sticking in some unfortunate animal), a replacement is already anchored firmly in position and ready to do business. This renewing of the fangs ex-

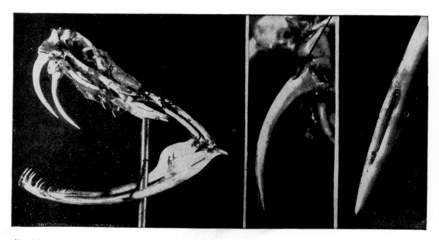

(Left) Skull of a PIT VIPER (*Fer-de-Lance*), with (center) an enlarged view of one fang (note wire threaded through the hollow), and (right) a greater enlargement showing the opening just above the fang's tip.

plodes the old belief that a poisonous snake can be rendered harmless by pulling its fangs out. In such a case the reptile would be temporarily less dangerous, but far from harmless, for some venom would be expelled in biting and the small, needle-like teeth of the lower jaws would surely produce lacerations through which venom could get into the blood.

The Timber Rattlesnake

The timber, or banded, rattlesnake, occurs over a large area of the eastern and central United States, being found from New England to northern Georgia and westward to Iowa and northeastern

Texas. Its place in the southeastern states and along the Gulf States is taken by a subspecies called the canebrake rattlesnake.

The average length of the timber rattlesnake is a little more than three feet, with four-foot specimens not uncommon in some localities. The maximum length appears to be six feet two inches (Ditmars [8]), but any specimen close to the six-foot mark would be considered a veritable giant of its kind. It is a rather stocky snake with a broad head that is very distinct from the neck and with scales that are strongly keeled.

This is a rather variable species so far as color is concerned, as there seem to be several color phases. The commonest phase is pale yellowish brown or yellowish gray, with a number of dark brown or black wavy cross-bands, very irregular in outline, but commonly pointed in the rear. Some individuals, especially females, are a light almost sulphur yellow, with irregular cross-bands that are scarcely darker than pale gray. Some specimens may be olive brown. As a matter of fact the ground color may vary from yellow to tan or black. The black specimens, which are not uncommon, have bands that are not discernible except in certain lights and from certain angles. These latter serpents are usually males. The tail is generally black, and the lower surface of the reptile is yellowish with numerous black spots and blotches.

The tail ornament, which gives this group of snakes its name, is a curious development confined to reptiles of this hemisphere. When a baby rattlesnake arrives in this world it bears on the end of its tail a rather delicate bulb or "prebutton." This structure is lost when the skin is first shed, exposing the button. The next time it sheds its skin it adds a horny segment next to the button, and every subsequent shedding adds another. These horny rings form under the skin and are exposed when the old epidermis is discarded. The rattle does not contain "beads," the peculiar whirr being produced by a rapid vibration of the whole tail when the loosely fitting rings rattle shrilly.

The rattle appears to be purely a weapon of defense. It is sounded when the reptile is irritated or excited. It might be pointed out that many other snakes, such as blacksnakes and pine snakes, vibrate their tails very rapidly under the same conditions, and if they chance to be among dead leaves, they too produce a rattling sound, but not the characteristic whirr of the rattler. The latter sound will never be forgotten once it has been heard.

This tail-shaking habit, then, is intended to serve as a warning, and undoubtedly has saved many a snake from being trodden upon by a steer, horse, or man. So far as the latter is concerned, how-

TIMBER RATTLESNAKE
Pale yellowish brown, with black cross bands.

ever, the trait has probably done more harm than good from the snake's viewpoint, for the explosive whirr has revealed the presence and brought about the ultimate destruction of many a rattler that would have remained safely hidden if it had kept quiet. If a rattlesnake is taken by surprise, it does not hesitate to strike first and sound its "buzzer" afterward; so it pays good dividends to depend on your eyes as well as your ears when in rattlesnake country.

The timber rattlesnake prefers to live in rocky and more or less mountainous areas that are rather well supplied with trees. It is the snake associated with the "snake dens" on rocky hillsides with southern exposures, where, in the early spring, one sometimes encounters large numbers of specimens basking in the warmth of the early season sun, often in the company of nonpoisonous snakes. During the dry season this snake wanders down to lower ground in search of food and water, but for most of the year it should be looked for in elevated situations where there is an abundance of ledges.

It is more even-tempered than most of our other rattlesnakes, and accidents involving the timber rattlesnake are remarkably rare, considering that this species occupies that part of our country that is most densely populated. This may be attributed to the reptile's gentle nature (for a rattlesnake), and to its preference for a home in regions that are of little use to man.

The timber rattlesnake feeds exclusively upon warm-blooded prey. Rats and mice, squirrels and small rabbits, and various birds make up its diet. Ordinarily the reptile strikes its victim and then lets go. The unfortunate animal may stagger for some distance, even for several yards, before paralysis sets in, but the rattler is always able to follow its trail at leisure and to locate it in plenty of time for dinner. Much of the snake's hunting, especially during warm weather, is likely to be done at night.

The timber rattlesnake does better in captivity than the majority of its relatives. It does not ordinarily have the sullen disposition of the eastern diamond-back, and it is not so excitable as the others. As a general rule it accepts food after a hunger strike of a few weeks, although some individuals will starve to death if they are not force-fed. It cannot be emphasized too strongly, however, that poisonous snakes should not be kept in captivity by the amateur. There is always the possibility of escape, and one little slip-up might cause a fatal accident. The beginner is urged to limit his snake-rearing activities, if any, to the non-poisonous reptiles.

The timber rattlesnake gives birth to living young. They are about nine inches in length and are few in number, usually from five or six to twelve. The newly born youngsters come equipped with tiny fangs and functional poison glands. They need to be treated with care.

In the coastal plain regions from southern Virginia to Florida, westward as far as Texas, and in the Mississippi Valley up to southern Illinois, we find a rattlesnake that is so much like the timber rattlesnake of more northern distribution that it cannot be called a different species, though it consistently differs enough from the northern form to be listed as a race of that reptile. This serpent is known as the canebrake rattlesnake.

It is a larger and stouter snake than the timber rattler, old individuals attaining a length of nearly seven feet. The color is pale gray, often with a pinkish tinge, and in addition to the irregular cross-bands there is commonly a rusty-brown line down the center of the back. This is a thoroughly dangerous reptile, showing a marked preference for marshy situations. It is to be found about the swamps, canebrakes, and low river bottoms where it feeds upon cotton rats, rabbits, muskrats, and occasionally on birds.

The Diamond-Back Rattlesnake

The diamond-back rattlesnake has the dubious honor of being the largest poisonous snake in this country. It might well be considered the most deadly snake as well, for while its venom may be no more potent than that of some of the other pit vipers, nevertheless the extra quantity of venom that a large specimen is able to inject makes this reptile potentially the most dangerous of them all.

The diamond-back is at home from North Carolina to Florida and westward in the Gulf States as far as Louisiana. It is a stout and heavy, big-headed serpent, averaging about five feet in length, though it gets to be much larger. Seven-foot specimens are rarely found. The record appears to be a specimen that measured eight feet nine inches (Stejneger [12]).

The snake is olive or grayish brown above, the upper surface decorated with a chain of large, diamond-shaped markings of dark greenish black. Each diamond, narrowly edged with pale yellow, encloses a patch of paler brown. The tail is barred with black and the lower surface is dull yellow. The sides of the head bear two

light-colored diagonal stripes, one in front of the eye and one behind it. The scales are heavily keeled.

The diamond-back rattlesnake is found in a variety of environ-
ments. It lives in the swamplands of the coastal regions where it
is sometimes seen voluntarily swimming in salt water. It is equally

DIAMOND-BACK RATTLESNAKE
Olive, with greenish black diamonds edged with white or pale yellow.

at home in the sandy pine barrens and on rocky ridges. It is a bold
and fearless reptile, and rare indeed is the individual specimen that
will back down when approached. The snake will not go out of
its way looking for trouble, but in the majority of cases a surprised
diamond-back will promptly assume a posture of defense, sound
its warning, and stay right where it is, making you go around *it*.
A six- or seven-foot specimen has fangs nearly an inch in length.

The snake does not have to be in a coil in order to strike, so it is important to exercise the utmost caution when on the home grounds of this reptile.

The diamond-back feeds exclusively upon warm-blooded prey. Despite the snake's fondness for swampy situations, it does not eat frogs or fish. Rabbits probably make up the bulk of its food, with birds, muskrats, and various small rodents comprising the remainder.

Like many other snakes, this one appears to do much of its prowling at night or just at sundown. During the heat of the day it is likely to remain contentedly coiled beneath a dwarf palmetto or under a fallen log. It is not uncommon to see their trails—single furrows on dusty roads that wind through the palmetto country—showing where they have crossed during the night, while people traveling these same roads during the day may never set eyes on a living specimen.

The diamond-back rattlesnake in captivity usually remains sullen and vicious. Its large size, deadly reputation, and belligerent attitude, however, combine to make it a popular reptile in collections and it often forms the prize exhibit of small zoos. The young are born alive. They are few in number, generally less than a dozen, and are about fourteen inches long at birth. These youngsters are usually pugnacious from the start and are fully capable of inflicting dangerous, even fatal, wounds if they are handled carelessly.

THE WESTERN DIAMOND-BACK RATTLESNAKE

This is not so large a reptile as the eastern diamond-back, nor is it so brightly colored. Its average length is about four feet or four and one half feet, with quite large specimens a little more than seven feet long. It is found in the hot and arid regions of the Southwest, from Arkansas to Texas and westward to southern California. It is often called the Texas diamond-back.

This serpent is gray or grayish brown in color, with darker diamond-shaped markings that are edged with white. The colors are pale and in many cases the snake presents a faded, washed-out appearance. The tail is strongly barred with black near its end. The head is broad and heavy and the scales are keeled.

This is the second largest venomous snake in this country. It might be rated as the second most dangerous but it would be more accurate to accord it first place, for it outranks all other snakes in the number of fatal accidents for which it is responsible. The

WESTERN DIAMOND-BACK RATTLESNAKE
Dusty gray, with darker diamonds edged with white.

western diamond-back is at all times a bold and fearless reptile, ready to strike upon the slightest provocation. Its record as a killer is largely due, however, to the snake's abundance over a large area and to the fact that in many instances a bitten person may find himself many miles from the nearest help. When struck by the Florida diamond-back one is pretty sure to be within at most an hour's drive to some place where he can be treated. But hospitals and doctors being far apart in many parts of Texas and Arizona, a person has to rely largely upon first-aid measures if he is to survive.

The western diamond-back is at home in the sun-baked, rocky hills that are so widespread in the Southwest. During the heat of the day it rests under some boulder or in the scant shade of a cactus. It comes forth at sundown to forage for food. After dark it comes down into the flatlands and basins where it searches for rabbits, desert rats, and other rodents.

In 1941 the writer spent about a month in western Texas doing geological work in the Glass Mountain area. Each day was spent in the foothills, roaming over rocky country that was ideal for rattlesnakes. During that time not a single rattler was seen. Nearly every morning, however, from one to three crushed bodies were to be seen on the roads leading to the foothills, mute evidence of the snake's abundance after dark. Experiments have shown that one of these inhabitants of the sun-drenched hills will die if forced to remain for an hour in the direct glare of the midday sun.

The western diamond rattlesnake is moderately hardy in captivity but it is usually a cross-tempered brute that does not always bother to rattle before it strikes. The young, born alive, are not many in number, usually fewer than fifteen.

THE PRAIRIE RATTLESNAKE

This is a fairly sizable serpent, averaging between three and four feet in length, large specimens attaining a length of about five feet. It is a reptile of the West, ranging over nearly all the country west of the Mississippi River. With such a wide distribution the prairie rattlesnake has been divided into several races or subspecies, of which the typical form, the true prairie dweller, occurs from the Mississippi River to the Rocky Mountains and from southern Canada to Texas.

This snake is often rather slender, as rattlesnakes go, although some individuals may be quite chunky. The color is yellowish brown and the back is decorated with large, rounded blotches of dark brown, each separated by a bit of the ground color. Toward the tail the blotches tend to form bands. The sides bear smaller blotches, and the lower surface is greenish yellow. The scales are keeled, as they are in all rattlesnakes.

The prairie rattler, living in the flat grasslands where there are not many rocky crevices to slink into, has its den in the ground. It very commonly takes up residence in an old prairie-dog burrow, and this fact has given rise to the oft-told story about rattlers and

PRAIRIE RATTLESNAKE
Yellowish brown, with dark brown blotches.

prairie dogs living amicably together. Another common inmate of prairie-dog towns is the burrowing owl, so that creature was also included in the tale, and the bird, reptile, and mammal were said to live together in an admirable spirit of good-fellowship. Actually the bird and rodent take pains to keep a respectful distance between themselves and any of the rattlers.

The food of this rattlesnake is composed chiefly of rodents, which abound on the prairie. The young, born alive as with the other rattlesnakes, average about twelve in a brood. The prairie rattler is said to strike more quickly and with less reason than the other members of its family. Perhaps more commonly than any other rattler, this one sometimes strikes without any warning rattle. Its record in the listing of snakebite fatalities of the whole country is second only to that of the bigger diamond-back from Texas.

In captivity this irritable serpent often becomes surprisingly docile, and because of this it is one of the best of its group for use

PACIFIC RATTLESNAKE
Yellowish brown to almost black, with darker blotches.

as an exhibition specimen. It usually takes food readily after a short preliminary fasting, is quite hardy in confinement, and actually acts good-naturedly—for a rattlesnake!

In the basin lands from Idaho and southern Oregon southward through Nevada and Utah there is a subspecies of the prairie rattler known as the Great Basin rattlesnake. This is a somewhat larger race, more at home in semidesert regions than the snake just described. On the Pacific Coast still another race flourishes. This is the Pacific rattlesnake, which lives in more or less forested areas as well as in open country. In snakes of this type the blotches are in many cases less rounded than with the typical prairie rattlesnake, and the general colors are more variable. Some individuals are almost black. The Pacific rattlesnake is the only poisonous snake found on the west coast north of southern California. It ranges northward to British Columbia.

THE SIDEWINDER

The sidewinder, or horned rattlesnake, is a relatively small serpent. Its average length is about one and one half feet, with large specimens somewhat in excess of two feet. A reptile of sandy wastelands, it is found in the desert areas of southern California, Nevada, Utah, and Arizona.

This snake is not hard to recognize for it has a pair of short, hornlike projections above its eyes. It spends a large part of its time lying half-buried in the sand, awaiting the approach of some unsuspecting lizard or rodent. It has been suggested that these projections may help to keep the sand from drifting into the snake's eyes. The serpent's color is yellowish gray or sandy brown, harmonizing perfectly with its surroundings, and its back bears a series of dull, irregular blotches. A few dark bands adorn the tail. The body is quite stout. The scales are strongly keeled, those along the dorsal line having sharply raised, almost tubular midribs.

The remarkable feature concerning this snake is its manner of locomotion. The sidewinder is perfectly able to crawl in a straight line like any other rattlesnake, but when in a real hurry it travels in a manner unlike any other American serpent. On very smooth, flat surfaces, however, other snakes may approach sidewinding. The reptile progresses in a sideways manner, or so it appears to the eye. A loop of the body is thrust forward to one side of the head, and as one loop follows another in rapid succession the snake seems to be skipping off in the direction towards which its head is pointed. The sidewinder almost gives the impression that it is jumping sideways or "rolling," and its tracks are evenly spaced furrows that curve in the sand. This odd manner of progressing is certainly the most efficient for a snake with a relatively short body when traveling in loose sand. It is worthy of note that some two or three desert-dwelling vipers of Africa have developed the same method of locomotion.

The sidewinder, with its method of locomotion so perfectly adapted for efficient progression over sand, literally rolls along with its body making little more than two contacts with the sand. Oblique, disconnected, parallel tracks are formed as the weight of the snake is carried progressively from one contact to the next, each point on the body behind the head being carried through an S-shaped path above the ground as the snake moves forward. This leaves on the sand an imprint of each scale on the body behind the neck, with the tail dragging to form a hooked-shaped imprint on the end of a straight track. From these imprints it would seem as though the snake had been lifted and replaced on the sand.

All the rattlesnakes so far discussed belong to a single genus, *Crotalus*. We have two other slightly different rattlers in this country, generally referred to as pigmy or ground rattlesnakes, although the latter term is somewhat misleading since all of the rattlesnakes are ground-dwelling serpents. The chief point of difference between these two groups has to do with the tops of their heads. With the two rattlesnakes that we are to take up next, the head is covered with large, symmetrical plates arranged in a manner not unlike those of a harmless snake. All the other rattlesnakes have the top of the head covered with small scales instead of plates.

THE MASSASAUGA

The larger of these ground rattlers is called the massasauga. It is also known as the swamp rattlesnake, as it shows a marked preference for swampy or boggy territory. There are two subspecies, called the eastern massasauga and the western massasauga, and combined they range from western New York to Nebraska and from southern Canada to Oklahoma and Arizona.

This snake, which averages a little over two feet in length, is usually quite stout. The color is gray or brownish gray, with a series of oval, black blotches on the back, each blotch well separated from the next and edged with white. The sides bear two rows of smaller blotches, and the underside is dark gray heavily splashed with black. The scales are strongly keeled. Occasional specimens are nearly black all over, with the dorsal blotches scarcely discernible.

MASSASAUGA
Brownish gray, with black blotches that are edged with white.

As has been suggested, this reptile prefers marshy country as a rule and does most of its prowling in wet meadows and swampy fields. It is largely nocturnal, but is often encountered on overcast or rainy days. As one might guess from its choice of habitat, it is fond of frogs, but it is believed to feed chiefly upon meadow mice.

The massasauga is usually rather slow to anger and is less likely to strike without good reason than the other rattlesnakes. So far as the writer has been able to determine, there are no authentic records of death from the bite of this snake, but it should be regarded and treated as a potentially deadly serpent nonetheless as its venom has been proved to be highly toxic.

The massasauga is not a very common snake at the present time. It appears to be unable to hold its own in settled regions, and is now moderately rare over much of the territory it formerly roamed, although it persists quite well in some areas. It takes to captivity rather better than the majority of its family, seeming to lack the viciousness of most rattlesnakes. The young, which are born alive late in the summer, average about ten to a litter.

THE PIGMY RATTLESNAKE

The other member of this group of rattlesnakes having plates instead of scales on the top of the head is a diminutive fellow only about eighteen inches long, appropriately known as the pigmy rattlesnake. This little reptile lives from the Carolinas to Florida and westward to Texas and Oklahoma, the territory being shared by three subspecies.

The snake rarely exceeds two feet in length, but it is relatively stout. The color is ashy gray, with a series of large, rounded, well-separated blotches along the back and two or three rows of smaller ones on the sides. There may be a rusty stripe between the dorsal blotches. The underside is yellowish white, heavily marbled and splashed with black.

The pigmy rattler is not so much of a marsh lover as the snake just described. It is sometimes found in swampy country as it is very interested in frogs from a dietary viewpoint, but as a rule one should look for this snake in dry, sandy areas. It is not so mild-mannered as the massasauga, and is generally a spunky and easily irritated snake. It has a diminutive rattle that can be heard for only about ten feet.

The pigmy rattlesnake is the least dangerous of our pit vipers. This is due largely to its small size, but partly because its venom is less virulent. This snake should not be treated with contempt, however, for a well-placed bite could very probably prove fatal if treated with indifference.

The chief food items of this reptile are mice, frogs, lizards, and small snakes. The young, which come in small broods of about ten on the average, are slightly less than six inches long at birth. One brood of eighteen has been recorded.

It is interesting to note that these two ground rattlers have head plates that might suggest some remote relationship to the copper-

PIGMY RATTLESNAKE, SHOWING THE UNDERSIDE
Gray, with darker blotches. Sometimes rusty on the back.

head and the water moccasin. Both of these latter pit vipers have the characteristic head plates, and both feed commonly upon frogs. Frogs are eaten regularly by the pigmy rattlesnake and the massasauga, but are consistently refused by all the other rattlesnakes.

THE COPPERHEAD

The copperhead is a moderately robust, rather handsomely marked snake, usually less than a yard in length. The record appears to be a specimen that measured four feet five inches (Ditmars [8]). There are three recognized subspecies, and together they range from central New England to northern Florida and westward to Texas and Illinois.

COPPERHEAD

Pale grayish brown, with dull to bright orange-brown wavy bands.

This is a "two-toned" snake; the two contrasting shades of brown have been compared to the contrast between an old copper penny and a shiny new one. The ground color is pale grayish brown, and on this is laid a pattern of rich chestnut cross-bands. The bands are broad on the sides and much narrowed where they cross the back so that when looked at from above they suggest the outlines of hourglasses. The head is moderately large and usually of a paler shade than the body, often having a coppery tinge. The underside of the snake is pinkish gray with a row of dark spots on each side of the belly. The scales are keeled.

The copperhead has a number of popular names. In various parts of the country it is known as the red adder, deaf adder, highland moccasin, and chunkhead. It prefers to live in upland country and is generally found on rocky hillsides in the vicinity of ledges or stone quarries. During dry spells, especially in the late summer, it frequently moves down and haunts grassy meadows and the weedy borders of ponds in search of frogs, but for the most part one thinks of the copperhead as a reptile of dry, timbered regions.

The writer has had his best success in searching for this snake while poking around in the old sawdust and slab piles left over from some lumbering operation of the past. Such places are commonly found in many sections where the timber was cut off many years ago, and there are likely to be several heaps of rotting planks and bark scattered about among the second-growth trees. These heaps provide ideal conditions for wood mice, and where the mice congregate one is likely to find rodent-eating snakes, including the copperhead. When examining a slab pile of this sort, it is hardly necessary to remind the reader that he must use utmost caution. To reach down and pull out or overturn slabs or bark with your bare hands is sheer recklessness as there may be a copperhead or a rattlesnake lurking under any one of them. While neither reptile is ordinarily aggressive, they could hardly be blamed for striking in self-defense if suddenly so disturbed. Use a long pole, perhaps with a hook nailed to one end, for this sort of work.

The copperhead will retreat if it has an opportunity to do so, or it will "freeze" in position and trust to its protective coloration to avoid detection. It might be noted that the snake's pattern is remarkably like sunlight falling on dead leaves. As a consequence, a quiet copperhead in the forest is often astonishingly hard to see. The reptile's fangs are shorter than those of a rattlesnake of the same size, and its venom is not rated as being so potent as that of the rattler. Serious accidents involving the copperhead are not common, and most people that are bitten recover with only a painful period of suffering. This is not to suggest that the copperhead is not a dangerous serpent. It is, and it should be so considered by anyone who is collecting, studying, or photographing snakes.

The copperhead is not at all choosy about its food. Almost any living thing that can be swallowed is acceptable. Mice, other small mammals, and birds are on its principal bill of fare, but it will eat

COPPERHEAD

frogs, lizards, and other snakes and is very fond of certain insects. The larvae of our larger moths are devoured, especially in the late summer when those of the sphinx-moth group are seeking favorable places to pupate in the ground. Stomach examinations have revealed the presence of many other insects, notably seventeen-year cicadas.

The copperhead has living young, usually no more than ten at a time. The youngsters are marked like their parents but the last half inch or so of their tails is bright yellow. It has been suggested that with the young snakes resting quietly among dead leaves, only the tail tip would be plainly visible and by wriggling it enticingly a wood frog or peeper might be attracted to within striking distance, believing it to be some kind of grub. The yellow color disappears by the time the young copperhead is a year old.

The Water Moccasin

The water moccasin or "cotton-mouth" is a snake of the southern swamplands, at home from Virginia to Florida, in the Gulf States, and northward in the Mississippi Valley as far as southern Illinois.

WATER MOCCASIN

The young are gray, with greenish brown wavy bands. The adults are a dingy greenish brown.

Moccasins are frequently reported from ponds well north of this range, even from New England, but such occurrences invariably turn out to be merely extra fat and ugly water snakes.

This, the dreaded snake of southern swamps and bayous, is fully as aquatic as any water snake. It averages a little over three and

one-half feet in length, the record standing at four feet ten inches
(Ditmars [8]). It is a very stout and heavy reptile with a large and
broad head and a short tail. Young specimens are rather brightly
colored, with a pale reddish brown ground color and a pattern of
irregular, wavy, darker cross-bands, each narrowly edged with
white. The pattern strongly suggests that of a copperhead, which
is not strange, as both snakes belong to the same genus. After the
moccasin gets to be partly grown the pattern tends to fade and

YOUNG WATER MOCCASINS
Gray, with greenish brown wavy bands.

become indistinct, and in old specimens the cross-bands are usually
completely gone, the reptile being a uniform dirty brown or black.
The lower surface is pale yellow with brown blotches. The inside
of the mouth is white. When the snake is disturbed it commonly
faces its enemy and opens its mouth wide, displaying the white
interior—hence the popular name of "cotton-mouth." The scales
are strongly keeled.

The water moccasin will eat birds and small mammals, and
during the course of a year will undoubtedly consume a large number of young ducks, marsh rabbits, young muskrats, and other
creatures that inhabit its aquatic surroundings. Its chief food, however, appears to be frogs and fish. The moccasin is not so lively as

the water snakes. It spends a large part of its time lying half concealed at the water's edge, patiently waiting for some unsuspecting victim to approach close enough for grabbing purposes. Being a fair climber, it often basks on some branch that overhangs the water. Like many of our other snakes it is as likely to hunt at night as during the daytime.

ADULT WATER MOCCASIN
Dingy greenish brown.

When surprised at the edge of some pond or river, a water snake will hurl itself into the water, sometimes with a great splash, and seek safety in its depths. But not so the moccasin. In most cases the poisonous snake will merely tighten its coils, erect its head, and open wide its mouth, warning you to keep your distance. The venom of the water moccasin is reported less virulent than that of the copperhead or rattlesnake, but since many moccasins are large enough to inject a rather large dose the snake is rightly regarded as being highly dangerous.

Although irritable and belligerent in the wild, the water moccasin generally becomes very tame and docile in captivity. It will live contentedly for years in confinement, accepting fish or frogs or mice, even strips of raw beef, with little hesitation. This species was rated by the late Dr. Ditmars [8] of the New York Zoological Park as the hardiest of all snakes in captivity.

It must be emphasized again, however, that neither this snake, the copperhead, nor any other venomous snake should be kept alive by an untrained person. A snake can squeeze through a surprisingly small crevice, and most individuals are past masters in finding some weak corner in their cage. With a harmless snake this is only mildly annoying, but with a poisonous one it can very easily result in tragedy.

THE CORAL SNAKE

We now come to the last of the poisonous snakes in this country, a relatively small, innocent looking, and really beautifully colored serpent that is generally rated the most deadly of them all. These are the coral snakes, of which we have two species, the best known one living from the Carolinas to Florida and westward to Texas and southern Illinois. The other is a smaller reptile, found in Arizona.

The first-mentioned coral snake is a rather slender serpent, averaging a little more than two and one-half feet in length. The maximum size appears to be represented by a thirty-nine-inch specimen (Ditmars [8]). The body is quite cylindrical, and the head is small and bluntly rounded, with practically no neck constriction. One look at this snake and you feel sure that it is a burrowing species.

The coral snake is ringed with red, yellow, and black, much the same as the scarlet snake previously described. In this case the nose is black, there is a yellow band just back of the eyes, and this is followed by a broad black band. Thereafter the snake is decorated with broad bands of black and red, each separated by a narrow ring of yellow so that the red and yellow are in contact, a condition never present with the nonpoisonous varieties or "mimics." The rings completely encircle the body. On many specimens there are irregular black dots in the red bands. The tail is ringed with yellow and black, with the red missing. The scales are smooth.

The coral snake belongs to the same family group as the cobras of Asia and Africa. Its venom acts quite differently from that of our other poisonous snakes, the pit vipers. Though the venom

CORAL SNAKE
Red, yellow, and black rings. The snout is black.

of a rattlesnake, moccasin, or copperhead attacks and breaks down the red blood cells, that of the coral snake attacks and paralyzes the nerve centers.

In spite of this reptile's deadly reputation, which is well deserved, accidents involving the coral snake in this country are remarkably uncommon. This can be attributed to several factors. In the first place the snake is a burrower by nature and is seldom encountered above ground. Specimens are occasionally discovered while plowing, and in the fall of the year, while harvesting the sweet potato crop, several individuals are usually uncovered. The snake is some-times found under logs or stones, but generally speaking a person might spend a lifetime roaming the southern woodlands without ever seeing an example of this colorful species.

Secondly, the coral snake has fairly short teeth. It is not equipped with long, movable fangs like the pit vipers, but is pro-vided with a pair of short venom-conducting teeth that are rigidly set in the upper jaw and are permanently erect. Ordinary clothing affords a fair measure of defense against these teeth unless the snake succeeds in striking a person on the hand or some other uncovered part.

The third reason for the low accident record of this potentially dangerous snake, and perhaps the deciding factor, is the fact that it is generally mild mannered and slow to anger. Many are the tales of children and unsuspecting adults that have picked up and handled one of these gayly colored serpents, entirely unaware that they were holding one of this country's most deadly reptiles, and the snake has shown not the slightest indication of biting.

This is *not* to say that the coral snake can be picked up with im-punity. The person who trusts to its good nature and picks up a specimen with his bare hands is being foolishly reckless, for the temperament of individual snakes varies and now and then we find a coral snake that will strike viciously. Usually, if the snake is going to bite, it simply reaches around and grabs hold without any pretense of the lightning-like strike of most snakes. But whether the coral snake strikes or merely "grasps," once it gets a grip on its enemy it retains that grip and starts chewing, imbedding its short fangs deeper and deeper. The coral snake, then, is a terribly dan-gerous snake, and despite any stories you may hear about the snake's unwavering mild disposition, each and every one that is discovered should be treated for precisely what it is, an extremely dangerous serpent.

The chief food of the coral snake appears to be lizards, other snakes, and probably salamanders. Not very much is known about its breeding habits aside from the fact that it lays eggs, usually few in number.

Our other coral snake, occurring in Arizona, is a smaller serpent, apparently never exceeding two feet in length. In this species the yellow bands are wide, often wider than the red ones, and the first color band behind the yellow of the head is red instead of black as in the larger coral snake of the Southeast. The Arizona reptile is presumably just as deadly as its eastern relative. There is not very much authentic information available on this secretive, semiburrowing snake, which is not often seen above ground.

First-Aid Treatment for Snakebite

In considering the most efficient manner of treating the bites of poisonous snakes, perhaps the first rule might be the old proverb, "An ounce of prevention is worth a pound of cure." The majority of snakebites are on the hands or forearms or on the lower part of the legs, and this fact suggests ways and means of avoiding such accidents.

Leather hiking boots that reach well above the calf of the leg are pretty good insurance against most of the poisonous snakes to be found in this country. If the trousers are worn outside the boots instead of tucked inside, the protection is greatly increased. When climbing up a steep rocky or wooded slope, never reach up for a handhold on some ledge or tree root until you have made certain that no serpent is lurking there, for the snake can scarcely be blamed for defending itself if it is suddenly confronted by a grasping fist. When overturning logs or stones, do so with a stout stick or pry bar, never with your bare hands. Snakebites in this country are not common, and a good many of those that do occur are the result of carelessness, accidents that could have been avoided if the person had taken sensible precautions.

If a person does have the misfortune to be bitten by a poisonous snake, there are certain first-aid measures that must be promptly taken. First of all, kill the snake in order to avoid a second bite, and identify it if possible in order to ascertain that it really is a venomous snake. There are many old-fashioned remedies ranging from chewing certain leaves to flooding the victim with whisky.

Each of these remedies has its staunch supporters among the rural population. The truth is that most of those who suffered no serious consequences after a whisky treatment, and who are loudest in its praise, have merely recovered from the bite of a blacksnake or a harmless water snake! It should be possible to identify a snakebite even if the snake escapes before you have had a good look at it. In the case of the pit vipers there are usually two small puncture wounds and nothing more. Sometimes there may be only one if the snake strikes a glancing blow or has one fang missing. All of the nonpoisonous snakes leave a series of small punctures or scratches, shaped something like a horseshoe.

Having ascertained that the bite is that of a poisonous snake, and that the reptile has been killed or driven off so there is no danger of another accident from the same source, a ligature or tourniquet should be applied just above the wound. This may be done with a belt, a necktie, or even with a shoelace. The object is to retard the spreading of the poison throughout the system. Do not have the ligature too tight, and do not leave it on for more than ten or twelve minutes. After that period loosen it for about one minute, then apply it for another twelve minutes.

The next step is to remove as much of the poison as you can. A surprisingly large percentage may be withdrawn by suction. The snakebite kits now sold in most sporting goods stores are provided with a small rubber bulb for this purpose. Lacking such an outfit it is perfectly safe to apply your mouth to the wound *provided* that you have no cuts or sores in your mouth or on your lips. The venom has to get into the blood in order to do any damage, and even if you inadvertently swallow a little in the excitement it will not do any harm.

After about fifteen minutes considerable swelling will have taken place in the vicinity of the bite. At this stage you should make an incision, using a razor blade sterilized by holding it in the flame of a match if no antiseptics are available. Cut a quarter inch or so deep, starting just back of one puncture and continuing through and a little beyond the other. Continue with the suction.

Potassium permanganate, burning gunpowder, and other substances used to be used for neutralizing the absorbed venom but it is now pretty generally agreed that such practices may do more harm than good. Antivenin is now available in most areas, and it is included in the snakebite kits just mentioned. This may be injected directly into the wound and the surrounding area. Generally speaking, antivenin should be administered by a physician or by someone else trained in its use. The antivenin outfit contains full directions which should be studied carefully by any person who intends to campaign in territory known to harbor dangerous snakes.

The really important thing to do is to get the patient to a hospital or to a doctor as quickly as possible, and that without any undue exertion on his part, for anything that causes the heart to beat faster pumps blood through the body more rapidly and this increased circulation speeds the spreading of venom throughout the system.

Chapter 8

NONPOISONOUS SNAKES OF OTHER LANDS

In considering the nonvenomous snakes of other lands, we shall begin with those that have always held a fascination for snake students and laymen alike, the big constricting serpents, the pythons and boas. No matter whether a person regards reptiles with admiration, fear, curiosity, or awe, these gigantic snakes are certain to excite some measure of genuine interest.

It is generally accepted that snakes developed from four-legged, lizardlike ancestors. In the pythons we find confirmation of this because of the presence of a pelvis and vestiges of hind limbs, the latter often in the form of clawlike spurs at the vent.

THE RETICULATED PYTHON

This species is believed to be the largest of all living snakes. As mentioned in the first chapter of this book, the length of a big snake is all too often exaggerated. There are many accounts of specimens exceeding fifty feet and even sixty, but there are no skeletons to confirm these measurements. The early Roman historian, Livy, recorded a serpent one hundred and twenty-five feet long that was eventually killed by a catapult of the Roman army, under Regulus, on the banks of the Bagrada River in Africa! The length of a snake, especially a stout one, is apt to be misleading. A python in an American zoo was estimated by its keepers to be about twenty-three feet long, but when it died and was measured it was found to be just under seventeen feet!

The reticulated python is known to attain a length of thirty-two feet, but very few individuals live long enough to reach this colossal size. The average length for a fully adult snake of this species is between fourteen and seventeen feet, and any specimen more than twenty feet in length can rightly be considered a large one. A twenty-five-foot python will weigh about two hundred and fifty pounds.

The head is uniform brown with a narrow black line in the center from the nose to the neck. The bewildering pattern of this snake is impossible to put down on paper. It may be described as

(New York Zoological Society Photo)

RETICULATED PYTHON

Iridescent, interweaving of rich yellows, browns, and blacks.

an interweaving of zigzag or X-shaped markings of rich yellow, brown, and black, the whole iridescent under certain lights. In a zoo this is a most conspicuous animal, but in its jungle home, with patches of sunlight splashed here and there among the tropical vegetation, the python melts into its surroundings perfectly.

The reticulated python is at home in the Philippines and throughout Burma, Indo-China, and the Malay Peninsula. The snake is not poisonous, but it can hardly be rated as not dangerous, for the squeezing power of a sizable specimen is almost unbelievable. Its food is composed chiefly of mammals and birds which it ordinarily captures by lying in ambush either among the tangle of vegetation on the jungle floor or entwined about the lower branches of some tree near a jungle path. It is a lover of water, as are most of the other big snakes, and it spends a lot of time partly submerged in forest pools. Captive specimens often stay in their water baths for days at a time.

The swallowing ability of this snake is usually exaggerated quite as much as is its length. It is estimated that a thirty foot python can swallow a hog of about one hundred and fifty pounds or an average-size white-tailed deer. The bulk of this snake's food, however, is composed of the larger jungle fowl and the young of various mammals, particularly wild swine and members of the deer and antelope families. Captive specimens are fed with rabbits, guinea pigs, small hogs, goats, and various fowls. The horns of a goat or small deer do not prove an obstacle; these are engulfed with the rest of the animal. If the horns should happen to pierce the stomach wall and skin, they fall off as soon as the skull has been digested. The python has proved many times that it is more than a match for the big leopard that lives in the same jungle, but it does not put on exhibitions of strength just for the fun of it. Most of its food is made up of relatively small and easily overpowered animals.

Regarding the reticulated python's ability to overpower a man, it may be stated that a ten- or twelve-foot individual can be dangerous if it succeeds in embracing a person's chest, especially if one of the arms is imprisoned and no help is within call. Against a python of over fifteen feet the most powerful man would be utterly helpless once the reptile had entangled him in its massive coils.

The python lays eggs about the size of goose eggs, sometimes as many as a hundred, and actually appears to incubate them! This seems contrary to all understanding of cold-blooded animals, but several times captive pythons have laid eggs and remained coiled about them until they hatched. Thermometers slipped between their coils have indicated that the snake's temperature was several degrees above that of companion snakes sharing the same cage. The young are about two feet long when hatched.

The temperament of individual reticulated pythons varies. They nearly all appear sluggish and lazy in captivity, generally showing evidence of interest in their surroundings only when hungry. Some specimens are irritable at such times, while others appear placid and calm on all occasions. But persons who are charged with the responsibility of caring for these big constrictors take no unnecessary chances and treat them all as potentially dangerous animals.

THE INDIAN PYTHON

On the mainland of India, in Ceylon, and throughout Burma and Indo-China there is a python somewhat smaller than the big reticulated python. This is the Indian python, also known as the

INDIAN PYTHON
Pinkish or yellowish gray, with black blotches.

Indian rock python and the black-tailed python, which reaches a maximum length of about twenty-five feet. It is usually considered the world's second largest serpent, although the South American anaconda might give it a race for that honor.

This python is another handsomely marked reptile, the ground color grayish or yellowish, sometimes even pinkish in juveniles. A series of large, oval, blackish patches are present on the back, each enclosing an area of the ground color. The sides are blotched and marbled with rich browns and grays, and in certain lights the reptile's body glistens with an iridescent bluish sheen. The lower surface is dull yellowish. One point of difference between this snake and the reticulated python is the fact that the Indian snake has a lance-shaped mark on the top of its head, while the crown of the larger python's head is decorated with a straight line.

The Indian python lives chiefly in jungle country. Like all the other pythons it has a prehensile tail. It is fully at home in trees, generally lying in wait for its quarry in the crotch of some vine-covered tree ready to dart abruptly down upon any passing game. It is also very fond of lying partly submerged in some forest pool. It feeds upon mammals, birds, and reptiles, showing a preference for mammals of relatively large size. Wild swine, small deer, and similar prey make up the bulk of its food. An eighteen-foot specimen has been known to overpower and swallow a full-grown leopard.

Despite this reptile's large size and tremendous strength, it is generally easygoing and lazy. Collectors report that even medium-size individuals can sometimes be grabbed and stuffed into collecting sacks without their making any effort to defend themselves. The snake's large size, beauty of pattern, and usual good nature combine to make it a great favorite with showmen. Few traveling carnivals fail to include an Indian python in their menagerie.

THE ROCK PYTHON

This is the largest serpent to be found in Africa. It is not so large a snake as the big pythons of India, generally averaging between sixteen and eighteen feet in length and probably seldom exceeding twenty feet. It occurs in central and southern Africa and chooses for its haunts the moist tropical jungles that alone provide secure retreats and an ample food supply for these gigantic snakes.

The color is pale brown, and the back is decorated with dark brown, more or less wavy, cross-bars that are black-edged and usually connected by an interrupted or continuous dark stripe running along each side. The upper surface of the tail has a pale streak between two black lines, and the serpent's lower surface is spotted and dotted with brown.

Small deer and antelope, large rodents, and jungle birds make up most of this python's food. The rock python is fairly common in American zoos. Its habits are essentially the same as those of its Asiatic relatives.

The Diamond Python

There are a few pythons in the far-off island of Australia, and perhaps the best known of these is the diamond python. This snake, which gets to be about sixteen feet in length, is a husky, handsome reptile. Its colors are quite variable, the common phase being dark brown on the upper surface, broken by blotches and elongated patches of pale gray or yellow. Sometimes these patches assume a diamond shape. The underside is usually pale yellow.

This python is at home in the wet jungle, where it feeds upon birds and mammals. It is a superb climber, and, like the other pythons the world over, delights in lying partly submerged in water. A race of this snake, with a particularly intricate and colorful pattern, is popularly known as the carpet snake or carpet python.

The Royal Python

The royal python, or ball python, is a little fellow, as pythons go, averaging only about five or six feet in length. A rugged and sturdily built reptile, it generally appears to be longer than it is. Its home is in western Africa.

This is a truly beautiful snake. The color is a rich reddish brown, with many irregular blotches of paler shade, each margined with yellow. There are numerous triangular or Y-shaped markings on the sides. Being a timid snake, it gets the name "ball python" from its curious habit of tucking its head out of sight inside its coils, which are tightened around the head in such manner that the snake becomes a compact ball. This the reptile does when it suspects there is danger afoot. When in this spherical condition it may be rolled along like a bowling ball! Dr. Ditmars [8] reported that the royal python is a snake of extreme gentleness. Most specimens cannot even be induced to bite.

THE WATER ANACONDA

The water anaconda or water boa, of South America, is a large constricting snake, the largest serpent in the New World. It is not so long as the Old World pythons, but it is a real giant nonetheless.

(New York Zoological Society Photo)

YELLOW ANACONDA

Greenish brown, with darker spots.

Its average length is well under twenty feet, and the largest specimen recorded appears to be just under twenty-five feet (Amaral [1]). The anaconda, however, is a much stouter and heavier reptile than any of the pythons. A specimen at the New York Zoological Park

measured nineteen feet in length, a full yard in circumference at
the thickest part of its body, and weighed two hundred and thirty-
six pounds.

The anaconda's color is deep greenish or olive brown, with a
double series of large, rounded, dark spots staggered on the back.
Smaller, white-rimmed spots are present on the sides, and the lower
surface is greenish gray.

This snake is at home in the well-watered tropical forests of
central South America. It is not a water snake and does not even
swim well, but it commonly submerges in some murky stream with
just its head floating on the surface and there waits for creatures
that come to drink. It feeds chiefly upon mammals—small deer,
agoutis, peccaries, capybaras, baby tapirs—and upon ducks, geese,
and other members of the bird world that frequent watery places.

In captivity the water anaconda is even more lethargic than the
pythons. Unlike the latter it does not lay eggs but instead gives
birth to living young.

In the Guianas and Venezuela of northern South America there
is another species, the yellow anaconda. This snake is smaller,
seldom exceeding fifteen feet in length. It is paler in color and
more heavily spotted.

The Boa Constrictor

The name "boa constrictor" has become popularly associated with
big snakes, and to most people all of the really large serpents are
"boa constrictors." Actually the name belongs only to a snake of
the American tropics that is not so large as many of the others.
This reptile seldom gets to be more than twelve feet long, but a
subspecies that occurs in Central America may attain a length of
eighteen feet.

The boa constrictor is a really handsome serpent. It is fairly
stout with a distinctly oval-shaped body, and is a powerful constrictor as its name implies. Like some of the pythons its coloration is hard to describe and quite variable. The back of some of
the more handsome individuals bears broad, elongate, saddlelike,

pale-gray blotches set on a background of rich chocolate brown. The sides, which are paler in tone, are decorated with dark brown spots that are often diamond shaped, with light centers. The tail is boldly marked with brick red and white. The underside is yellowish, dotted with black.

BOA CONSTRICTOR
Chocolate brown, with gray blotches. The tail is reddish and white.

This is a snake of well-watered, forested country. It is an accomplished climber and like most of the other big snakes it is also very fond of the water. Though its habits are largely nocturnal, it is often seen abroad during the day. It apparently feeds exclusively upon warm-blooded prey, but may eat some of the larger tree lizards. Its chief victims are monkeys, young peccaries, rabbits, and various other rodents, plus some of the larger jungle birds.

This is one of the commonest of large snakes in zoological parks and in traveling shows. The South American forms are usually very docile and mild mannered, seldom showing any signs of annoyance even when roughly handled. The somewhat darker variety from Central America is commonly more irritable, often hissing loudly and striking violently. A well-grown adult of either variety is powerful enough to kill a man if it gets him securely enveloped in its coils and if there is no other person to come to his assistance.

The boa constrictor has living young. They are nearly two feet long at birth and often come in large numbers. Partly grown examples of this snake often enter our country concealed in bunches of bananas. It is not at all uncommon in banana warehouses, where the fruit is hung up to ripen, to have a three- or four-foot boa constrictor drop onto the floor.

THE GREEN TREE BOA

The green tree boa is an interesting and highly colorful representative of medium-size constricting serpents that spend most of their time in the branches of trees. This species, which occurs throughout most of northern South America, is about four feet in length. The body is rather slender and the head is large and considerably swollen at the temples, giving the reptile a thoroughly dangerous look although it is perfectly harmless.

The color is brilliant green above with a pure white dotted line down the back and a number of narrow, widely spaced white cross-bars. The lower surface is pale yellow. In a cage this snake looks as conspicuous as a circus clown, but when coiled among the lush tropical vegetation the white markings serve to break the outlines of the green body. These markings mix with the small slits of sunlight that filter through openings in the foliage so that the snake in its native haunts is astonishingly hard to see.

Tree boas, of which there are several species, feed chiefly upon birds. In order to grasp and hold on to their feathered prey they are provided with extra long teeth, those in the front being almost fanglike in size. Most of the tree boas back up their formidable dentition with wicked tempers, strike savagely upon the slightest provocation, and are capable of inflicting deep and slashing wounds.

CUBAN BOA
Greenish, with white markings.

THE MANGROVE SNAKE

This is one of the most strikingly marked snakes of the Far East, where it occurs in the Philippines, Borneo, the Dutch East Indies, and in the Malay Peninsula. It is a graceful and well-proportioned snake, attaining a length of about seven feet. Its color is a rich, lustrous black, and the snake is decorated with numerous but widely spaced, narrow cross-bars of bright yellow. The underside is a deep bluish black.

This is a rear-fanged snake; its venom aids in slowing down struggling prey while it is being swallowed. As such it might be treated in the next chapter with the poisonous snakes of other lands, but since the mangrove snake is not generally considered dangerous to man we shall consider it with the other harmless or nonpoisonous reptiles. It is usually gentle and docile in captivity, and its striking colors make it an excellent exhibition specimen. With any serpent that has even mild poison glands, however, the keeper should always be on the alert and take no foolhardy chances.

The mangrove snake is strictly arboreal and diurnal, and though occasional individuals may be found on the ground, most of those observed are in trees. It feeds upon a variety of creatures, such as birds, mammals (including bats), lizards, tree frogs, and other snakes.

The Golden Tree Snake

The golden tree snake, sometimes called the black and gold tree snake, is a slender, elongate serpent about four and one half feet long, found from the Philippines to Sumatra and from southern China through Burma to India and Ceylon. The long body is somewhat compressed, the neck is sharply constricted, and the head is large with unusually large eyes. The plates on the snake's lower surface bear heavy, ridgelike keels on each side; these aid the reptile no little in climbing.

This is a bright and colorful snake. There are several color varieties, perhaps the best known being a bright greenish yellow, with each scale edged with black. In some cases the black is so disposed as to suggest cross-bars. There is often a series of orange or red spots along the back, and the underside is yellow, dotted with black.

As its name implies, this snake is arboreal in its habits. There are few reptiles that can compete with it in the tree tops. It feeds chiefly upon various lizards and is able to glide from branch to branch with marvelous dexterity. It is now a well-established fact that this snake can actually "leap" from one branch to another, and it is capable of "parachuting" to some extent. The peculiar keels on its belly scales enable the serpent to flatten the body and form a hollow trough of its ventral surface and sail downward at an angle. Experimenters who have dropped these snakes from a height of some twenty feet have discovered that instead of falling in a straight line the reptiles plane off at an angle, keeping their bodies rigid the whole time.

THE BLACK AND YELLOW RAT SNAKE

The black and yellow rat snake, sometimes called the spotted rat snake, occurs in tropical South America and ranges north through Central America to southern Mexico. Except for the large boas,

BLACK AND YELLOW RAT SNAKE—SOUTH AMERICA
Black, with lemon yellow bands.

this species is the largest nonpoisonous snake living in this hemisphere. It reaches a maximum length of nearly twelve feet, although most specimens are between six and eight feet long. The word "nonpoisonous" must be added to a description of this serpent because the deadly bushmaster also attains a length of about twelve feet.

The snake is rather slender but it is a strong constrictor, feeding upon rats and other small mammals as well as on birds and lizards. It is a strikingly marked reptile, jet black with narrow cross-bands of lemon yellow. On the forward part of the snake the yellow bands are diagonal, sloping towards the head, and in some cases are ill-defined, while towards the tail the serpent is banded with regularity. The lower surface is black, checked with white. The scales are smooth and very large.

This snake is usually good-natured in capivity. Freshly caught specimens will put up a battle, flattening the upper part of the neck vertically, but as a rule they soon calm down and become reasonably tame. The individual shown in the photograph was nearly seven feet in length. It arrived in New Haven, Connecticut, concealed in a shipment of bananas!

THE INDIAN RAT SNAKE

This is a large and slender snake, built along the general lines of our racers. Its length is usually given as eight feet, but since ten- and eleven-foot specimens have been recorded, this reptile may well be the longest nonpoisonous snake in the Far East, except, of course, the pythons. Its distribution is widespread, extending from Afghanistan through India, Burma, and Indo-China, and it occurs as well in the Malay Peninsula, Java, and Formosa. The natives of India call it the *dhaman*.

The prevailing color is olive brown, commonly without cross-bars except near the tail where the snake may be rather weakly banded with brown or black. Some individuals have suggestions of cross-bars for nearly their whole length. The lower surface is pale yellow, marked very regularly with black checks. One writer has likened the underside of this snake to a tape measure. The head is moderately long, the neck considerably constricted, and the slender but robust body is distinctly triangular in cross section, made so by a prominent dorsal ridge.

The Indian rat snake may be found in all sorts of territory, from swampy lowlands to dry and wooded highlands. Being an excellent climber, it is frequently found high in a tree. It also enters the water freely and swims well. It is most active during the daytime.

This large snake is not aggressive. It will usually try to escape by making full use of its well-known speed, but if a specimen is cornered it will fight savagely. In such an event the serpent will assume a defensive attitude, raise its head well off the ground, and flatten the neck vertically in a manner contrary to that of a cobra. Since the snake strikes upward, many travelers report that it very plainly aims at a person's face. Though the snake is not venomous, nevertheless with its long, sharp teeth it can inflict a nasty, tearing wound.

In spite of its common name the Indian rat snake feeds largely upon frogs and toads! It will eat rats and mice as well as young birds, for it is not at all choosy about its diet, which also embraces lizards, small turtles, bats, and other snakes, including those of its own kind. It subdues struggling prey with the same technique as that adopted by our common blacksnake, pressing its victim firmly against the ground with a loop of its own body.

THE WOLF SNAKE

Throughout many of the islands of the South Pacific, and on the mainland of Indo-China, Burma, and India, there is a small snake that is rather commonly found around dwellings. This is the wolf snake, a reptile some two feet in length. Its color is quite variable. In some cases the ground color is pale brown and the body is banded with yellow, most strongly near the head. In others the bands are totally lacking. Still others are darker brown, banded with white.

This little snake, which seems to enjoy living in the crevices of masonry, is a more or less regular inhabitant of most of the villages and settlements of the Far East. Its habits being nocturnal, it prowls about after dark in search of geckos and mice. During the day it remains hidden in crevices or under boxes and other objects in dark corners. Being a superb climber, it is often discovered up among the rafters or high on some cupboard shelf.

The wolf snake is a spunky little fellow. If it cannot escape easily, it will put up a creditable defense, striking repeatedly. The serpent is not poisonous, however, and it is too small to be taken very seriously.

The Checkered Keelback

The checkered keelback occurs in India, Burma, southern China, the Malay Archipelago, and Java. It is considered a very common snake in India. It is a rather stout water snake, growing to a length of about four feet. The head is large and broad, and the strong keels on the dorsal scales impart a ridgelike appearance to the reptile's back. The color, which is quite variable, is usually some shade of olive or yellow, checkered by a series of squarish dark spots. The underside is pearly white.

Though this snake is at home in rivers and ponds, it goes on overland journeys more commonly than American water snakes do and is sometimes found prowling at some distance from the nearest water. Its chief food items appear to be frogs and toads, but fish are also eaten. The snake, an accomplished swimmer, is unusually active and energetic on land. It is said to be capable of "jumping" clear of the ground.

The checkered keelback is not poisonous but it is one of the most vicious snakes in the Far East. When angry it will flatten the upper part of its neck like a cobra, only to a much lesser extent, and hurl itself savagely at its tormentor. Unlike many other water snakes, this one lays eggs. The broods are usually large, often of more than fifty. This snake has frequently been exhibited in American zoos.

The Granular Water Snake

The granular water snake, also known as the gray water snake and the rasp-scaled water snake, is just about as thoroughly aquatic as any serpent can be without being a sea snake. Living from India and Ceylon to the Philippines and New Guinea, it spends nearly all its time in the water. It is, in fact, rather awkward and helpless on land. It occurs commonly about river mouths and brackish estuaries and swims freely about in salt water, sometimes miles from shore.

The snake is brown with a series of buff-colored bands that sometimes merge on the back. Young specimens are vividly banded with black and buffy yellow in a zebra-like pattern, while old individuals are usually a uniform dull brown. About four feet in length, the rather heavy body is compressed, an obvious aquatic adaptation. The skin appears to be so large for its owner that it hangs in loose folds when the snake is hauled out on land, giving the reptile a particularly unpleasant look. The eyes are set well on top of the head, as are the nostrils also. The latter are unusually large and rounded, and the snake's front end has been likened to the muzzles of a double-barreled shotgun!

The snake has very granular or warty scales which are also present on the underside in place of the usual broad plates or scutes. As a result of this condition the granular water snake cannot crawl, as do most other serpents, but must hunch itself along in a clumsy fashion. It is most agile in the water, however, and feeds principally, if not entirely, on fish. The young, which are born alive, are few in number.

This ugly and evil-looking reptile, which is not poisonous, is said to have a surprisingly good disposition. Colonel Frank Wall, in *The Snakes of Ceylon,* reports that the fishermen of Bombay handle these snakes without fear when they get into their nets, and that the serpents make no attempt to bite.

THE DOG-FACED WATER SNAKE

This oddly named reptile is found in the coastal regions of India, Burma, the Malay Peninsula, and some of the other island chains in the South Pacific. The body is stout and roughened by heavily keeled scales. The lower jaw is considerably enlarged, which gives the snake a rather forbidding, doglike aspect. Though not a large snake, it averages between two and three feet in length, with a maximum of about four feet.

The color is light bluish gray above and buffy yellow below. The upper surface is crossed by weak bands, and the lower surface is heavily spotted with greenish black. There is a dark streak extending from the eye along the neck.

This, too, is a thoroughly aquatic snake, living mainly in the brackish water of estuaries and tidal rivers. It has the unusual habit of anchoring itself by the tail to some submerged branch, and then swinging about in the current on the lookout for fish, which form its entire source of food. The snake is a powerful swimmer but on land it commonly progresses with a looping, sideway motion, something like that of an American sidewinder.

The dog-faced water snake, an ugly looking customer if there ever was one, is really an inoffensive and mild-mannered fellow, seldom showing any evidence of anger. Most specimens will permit handling from the beginning. Although the snake is very mildly poisonous, it is considered harmless to man.

THE NIGHT SNAKE

There are several small- to medium-size snakes in the American tropics that are known as night snakes. They are rear-fanged serpents and mildly poisonous but they are not generally considered dangerous to man. The little spotted night snake would be a good example. This is a slender, rather big-headed reptile, with smooth scales and elliptical pupils in its eyes. Its average length is about twenty inches.

The color is a rich tan with a series of irregular, oval, brown blotches on the back, some of them arranged crosswise, so that from directly overhead the snake appears to be ringed. Smaller spots on the sides alternate with those on the back.

As its name indicates, this snake is most active after dark, at which time it hunts among the weeds and along roadways for lizards and small snakes. When it grasps its prey it holds on and chews, imbedding its short rear fangs. The victim is very quickly paralyzed. This is another snake that often migrates, involuntarily, arriving in this country in shipments of bananas.

NIGHT SNAKE—SOUTH AMERICA
Yellowish tan, with brown blotches.

THE RINGED SNAKE

This is the common grass snake, or "water snake," of England and Europe, where it ranges eastward to western Asia. It is the *Ringelnatter* of Germany. Large examples are about six feet long, but the average length is between three and four feet. The snake is quite variable in color, but usually the ground color is gray or olive brown above, with spots and transverse bands of darker shade. There is commonly a white or yellowish collar, usually divided in the middle, and behind this a black collar. The scales are keeled.

This serpent is found in grassy meadows, along wooded streams, and in overgrown fields, wherever water is plentiful. It swims with its head well above the surface, and when it catches a frog or a fish it usually crawls out on shore to swallow it. Though cold-blooded prey constitute its main food, it will occasionally eat birds or mice.

The grass snake is an inoffensive creature which rarely makes any attempt at biting. It is an egg-layer, depositing from ten to twenty eggs during the summer.

THE DICE SNAKE

The dice snake, or tessellated snake, is distributed from southern France to central Asia. About five feet in length, the serpent is olive brown above and may be nearly uniformly colored. Most specimens, however, are decorated with dark spots that are usually staggered on the back. The lower surface is blackish, marbled with white, and sometimes red.

This reptile is not so aquatic in its habits as the ringed snake just described. It is usually found on higher and drier ground where it hunts in the thickets and along stone walls for rodents, lizards, and similar prey.

THE SMOOTH SNAKE

The smooth snake is a comparatively little fellow, seldom reaching twenty inches in length. It is very common over much of Europe and occurs sparingly in the British Isles. The upper surface is generally brown, with a large dark patch on the neck and a paired series of dots extending down the back. The lower surface is bluish black.

Though this little snake is inclined to be spunky when cornered, it is entirely harmless. It frequents dry and stony locations and preys chiefly upon lizards, salamanders, and small snakes.

THE LEOPARD SNAKE

This is probably the handsomest of European serpents, its home being in the southern sections of that continent. Its average length is about three feet. The general color is rich mahogany red, mottled on the back with deep red blotches that are rimmed with black.

These blotches are usually arranged in a double row but they may broaden into transverse bands. Smaller, crescentic spots on the sides alternate with those on the back.

This is a constricting snake that chiefly feeds upon warm-blooded prey. Rats, mice, voles, and similar small game make up the bulk of its food. These are often supplemented by birds and their eggs, as the leopard snake is an accomplished climber.

THE FOUR-RAYED SNAKE

This, the largest European snake, sometimes attains a length of from six to seven feet. It lives in southern and southeastern Europe. It is a trimly built reptile, varying from olive brown to light tan in color, with four longitudinal dark lines extending the length of its body. This snake looks very much like the four-lined rat snake, or yellow rat snake, of our southern states.

An expert climber and a powerful constrictor, the four-rayed snake feeds upon rats, moles, small birds, lizards, and other snakes. Throughout the territory where it is found it is generally regarded as a useful reptile and a welcome ally of the farmer.

THE EGG-EATING SNAKE

Mention should be made of an unusual little snake found rather abundantly in Africa, the so-called egg-eating snake. This is a small reptile, averaging about two feet in length and never exceeding a yard. Its color is pale brown and there are three rows of roundish darker spots on the back. The pupil of the eye is elliptical. The serpent's scales are very strongly keeled.

This snake apparently feeds almost exclusively upon eggs, and although its body is not at all stout nevertheless it can engulf an ordinary hen's egg with ease. A series of bony processes extends from the neck vertebrae into the back of the throat, and these neatly slice the shell as the egg is swallowed, after which the shell is regurgitated. There are many snakes that commonly eat eggs, along with other items, and we have several in this country, but this little African snake has made a life business of it!

Chapter 9

POISONOUS SNAKES OF OTHER LANDS

Throughout the world, except in Australia, harmless snakes outnumber the poisonous ones by a margin of about five to one. This is speaking of species. If we were to consider individuals, the ratio would be much greater. In Australia the dangerous snakes outnumber the nonpoisonous ones, but in all other places a person is much more likely to encounter a nonvenomous serpent than he is to meet a venomous one.

The really dangerous snakes can be conveniently grouped under four major headings. The pit vipers, which predominate in the New World; the true vipers, which occur in Europe and Asia but whose center of distribution is in Africa; the sea snakes of the Indian and Pacific Oceans; and the elapids, a group that includes the dreaded cobras, kraits, and mambas, and which is nearly worldwide in distribution. Our coral snakes are members of this latter group, as are all the poisonous snakes of Australia.

For the purpose of getting acquainted with a few of the poisonous snakes of other lands, we shall consider first the elapids, next the true vipers, then the pit vipers, and last the sea snakes, although these marine serpents, abundant in the tropical waters of the South Pacific and Indian Ocean, are most closely related to the first group, the elapids.

THE INDIAN COBRA

This is the notorious *cobra de capello* of the Far East, where it is also known as the spectacled or hooded cobra. The typical race or subspecies is found in India, but other subspecies occur from the Punjab region to southern China and on many of the islands of the South Pacific and Indian Ocean. It is a rather large, cylindrical snake with smooth scales, attaining a length of nearly seven feet

144

with three or four feet as a fair average. The color is quite variable but is commonly pale or darker yellowish brown, sometimes dappled or variegated with lighter marks on the fore part of the body. The head is not very distinct from the neck, and when not excited the cobra looks very much like a harmless type of snake.

Whenever the cobra is alarmed or angry, it rears up until approximately one third of its body is in the air, faces its enemy, and by raising its extra-long forward ribs spreads the neck skin to form the famous "hood." With the typical Indian cobra the hood bears a dark spectacle-like mark on its back, but with many of the subspecies this decoration may be lacking or present only in the form of a broken black line or a pair of dots.

This is the reptile used by itinerant snake charmers throughout the East. When the charmer squats beside his basket and begins to play on his flute, the cobras rear up, spread their hoods, and assume a defensive attitude. He then begins to sway from side to side and the alert snakes follow every movement by swaying themselves. To the onlooker it appears as though the serpents were dancing to the music. Snakes, however, are totally deaf; the flute is simply a side light of the entertainment. The cobras are merely following the man's movements, ready to strike if necessary, and the success of the act depends on the man's remarkable skill in knowing just how far he can go before the snakes will strike. Professional charmers have to replace their "actors" frequently, as it does not take long for them to become accustomed to the routine, after which they are reluctant to perform their part of the show.

The cobras and their near relatives, the mambas and kraits, do not have the long, movable fangs that are characteristic of the vipers and pit vipers. Instead, they have shorter fangs that are more or less rigidly fastened in the upper jaw, where they are permanently erect.

The bite of the cobra is regarded as being very dangerous and may prove to be fatal, although there are plenty of records of individuals who recovered from its effects. The Indian cobra is commonly regarded as the greatest killer among snakes, and while the greatest number of deaths from snakebite may occur in that country, it is probable that quite another serpent, Russell's viper, to be discussed later, is responsible for more than half of the total.

There are several reasons for the high death rate in India, although the frequently quoted "twenty thousand a year" is certainly open to question and is not accepted by modern authorities. A very high percentage of the people of India go about barefooted, and the cobra shows a decided liking for living (especially during the rainy season) about old buildings and even under the floors of native huts. Although the reptile is often encountered in the daytime, its habits are chiefly nocturnal, as are the habits of Russell's viper, so it is inevitable that the prowling snakes and the unprotected limbs of the natives frequently meet! To further complicate things in the snakes' favor, many of the Hindus have religious restrictions against killing any living creature; they would no more think of slaying a deadly snake than they would of doing away with their parents.

THE EGYPTIAN COBRA

There are two species (plus several subspecies) of cobra in the Asiatic region, but in Africa we find several different members of this hooded group. Perhaps the best known is the Egyptian cobra, or asp, which is found not only in Egypt but is more or less common throughout eastern Africa all the way down to the southern end of the continent.

This is supposedly the serpent used by Cleopatra for ending her life in the year 30 B.C. Its maximum length is about six feet, with the average specimen measuring under five feet. Its color is usually pale brown or olive yellow. But since the species has such a wide distribution there is bound to be considerable variation, and the asp may range from light tan or straw color to deep brownish black. The hood is well developed and sometimes decorated with dark marks but it lacks the spectacular eyelike markings of the Indian cobra. The underside of the snake is pale yellow, the scales are smooth, and the general appearance of the reptile is dull and lusterless.

The Egyptian cobra is not a jungle snake. It shuns the humid districts and lives in relatively dry and open regions especially where sandy stretches are interspersed with scrubby grasslands. It is a nervous and easily enraged snake, spreading its hood and striking

(New York Zoological Society Photo)

CAPE COBRA
Brownish black.

at the slightest provocation. It is not an easy snake to keep in healthy condition in captivity. This species is used by the snake charmers of Egypt in much the same manner as the Indian cobra is used by the Asiatic snake charmers.

The Spitting Cobra

The spitting cobra is a large and robust snake, attaining a length of about seven feet. It, too, enjoys a wide distribution, being found from upper Egypt south to the Transvaal. This reptile, however, prefers a more moist and shady environment than the others. As with many snakes that range over a considerable territory, there is much variation in color. This species varies from dull pinkish to slaty black, with all shades of olive, brown, and yellowish gray. The light-colored specimens have a broad band on the throat, while the black or dark-hued specimens commonly have a pair of reddish or yellowish patches that are visible on the spread hood.

This is one of the most dangerous snakes in Africa. Its large size, deadly poison, and commonly aggressive nature combine to make it a reptile to fear. And as though this were not enough, the snake has the peculiar habit of spitting at its enemy. Spitting is hardly the right term to use, as the cobra really ejects its venom in two fine jets, much as though a pair of water pistols were discharged in one's face. A large specimen can shoot this spray with remarkable accuracy for about eight feet. The serpent aims at its enemy's eyes, and many a jungle hunter has been taken completely by surprise when one of these snakes reared up out of the tall grass and suddenly let go. Temporary blindness, accompanied by excruciating pain, is the usual result of such an experience. If the eyes are not promptly and thoroughly washed with plenty of clear water, the blindness may be permanent. There is little doubt but that the jungle carnivores have learned to leave this well-equipped snake strictly alone.

THE RINGHALS

The ringhals or keeled-scale cobra is found in South Africa. It is the smallest of the cobras, seldom exceeding four feet in length. The color is brown above, sometimes banded with darker and blackish below, with one or two whitish bars on the throat. It is the only cobra having keeled scales.

This is another spitting cobra that follows exactly the same procedure as its larger relative just described. This snake's smaller size makes it less formidable, but collectors in the brush country of South Africa need to use care in bending over to poke in stone piles or around tangled undergrowth or they may get a dose of this reptile's venom full in the face.

The late Doctor Ditmars,[8] in charge of reptiles at the New York Zoological Park, reported that it was necessary to remove their two ringhals from their cage every five or six days to clean the glass, it being so thoroughly sprayed by the snakes' spitting at visitors that it was hard to see through it. This continued for a full half year before the cobras finally became accustomed to crowds of people.

Unlike the other cobras, the ringhals gives birth to living young. They generally come in large litters, sometimes as many as sixty at a time.

The King Cobra

The king cobra might be considered the world's most dangerous snake. It is far and away the largest poisonous snake in the world, attaining a length of about eighteen feet, with an average length of between ten and twelve feet. It is a relatively slender serpent, no bigger round than a rattlesnake half its length, but being very strong and rugged it is justly feared by all who live or travel in its native country. The king cobra inhabits South China, Burma, the Malay Peninsula, and many of the neighboring islands, including Borneo, Java, and the Philippines.

The general color is pale to dark yellowish brown, with or without numerous paler cross-bands. The head is usually several shades darker than the rest of the body and is commonly tinged more or less with dull orange on the chin. The scales are smooth, and the snake has a dull, satiny appearance. The hood of the king cobra, which the reptile spreads when it is enraged, is narrower than the hood of smaller cobras, and it bears no spectacles or other marks.

This deadly reptile is at home in the thick and tangled jungle as well as in relatively open country. It commonly haunts the banks of streams and is a good tree climber. When an average-size individual rears up in defense or for an attack, its head is pretty close to the same height as the head of a man. The snake's large size enables it to inject an unusually large amount of venom at a single bite, and the venom of the king cobra is as highly toxic as that of almost any other known snake. Coupled with these facts, the king cobra is one of the few snakes in the world that is known to make unprovoked attacks upon man. Several other poisonous snakes, notably some of the mambas, will occasionally move to the attack, especially if they are teased or tormented, but the king cobra is known for rearing up out of the grass and going for a man upon sight. A person unfortunate enough to be bitten by one of these reptiles has small chance of recovery.

KING COBRA—INDIA

Yellowish brown, with paler bands. Head and neck are darker. Old specimens are dark brownish.

The king cobra feeds largely, probably almost exclusively, upon other snakes. Captive specimens usually refuse all other food, and it is interesting to note that they generally refuse to accept American poisonous snakes, such as moccasins, although they promptly attack and devour the ugly southern water snakes. This suggests that in the wild state this snake, for all its title of "king," may avoid encounters with venomous species and content itself largely with nonvenomous prey.

The Mamba

The mambas are snakes that are celebrated in tales about jungle life in Africa. They are harmless appearing snakes, very slender and whiplike in build, with small heads; they do not at all fit the general conception we have of dangerous snakes. They are exceedingly poisonous, however, and they back up their venomous fangs with a nature that is at times bold and audacious.

There are at least five species of mamba in the Dark Continent. Best known of these is the South African mamba which occurs from the Ethiopian region south to Natal. There are actually two species, long confused or believed to be color phases. One of these is a beautiful green and the other a deep greenish blue or slaty black. This latter, the notorious black mamba, may approach fourteen feet in length. The green species seldom exceeds eight feet.

The mambas being superb climbers, it is doubtful if any snake anywhere can equal them in getting about in bushes and treetops. An alarmed specimen can glide from branch to branch, drop to the ground, dart across an open space, and ascend another tree, all so fast that the eye can scarcely follow it. The serpent actually appears to flow through the foliage.

The mamba has short fangs; they are situated in the extreme front of the upper jaw where they will be imbedded at the slightest nip. The snake is sometimes aggressive, probably chiefly during the mating season, and many are the tales of mambas lying concealed in the bushes and vines near jungle paths and darting like arrows at passing natives. Since a goodly percentage of mamba bites are likely to be on the face or neck, its record as a killer stands very high among venomous snakes.

The Banded Krait

The kraits are slender, trimly built snakes that inhabit the Far East. Having large, smooth scales, the general appearance of these reptiles is glossy and attractive. Like the mambas of Africa they appear to be harmless snakes, but their venom is rated very nearly as toxic as that of the cobras. There are several different species, the best known being the common banded krait which lives on the islands of Borneo, Java, and Sumatra, as well as on the Asiatic mainland.

This serpent, which averages from four to five feet in length, has a prominent ridge running down the center of its back. The color is pale yellow, often banded or ringed with brownish bands that are quite broad although there is considerable variation in individual specimens.

The kraits, which are nocturnal wanderers, often find their way into houses while searching for lizards or mice. As a result they are sometimes stepped upon, so they too add to the annual death rate from snakebite in the Asiatic region. The banded krait does not confine itself to lizards and rodents but will also eat frogs, birds, and other snakes.

Kraits are usually found in grassy fields and low scrubby jungle. Unless actually trodden upon the snake is not likely to bite. It is usually described by people who have studied it in its native haunts as a timid snake. Its nature is inoffensive, and captive kraits will generally refuse to strike until they have been subjected to prolonged teasing.

THE TIGER SNAKE

This reptile is generally regarded as the most dangerous snake in Australia. It is a husky serpent, attaining a length of nearly ten feet, although the average length is closer to five or six feet. The head, which is rather large, is distinct from the cylindrical body. The scales are smooth. Its venom is considered as deadly as that of any other known snake, and its temperament is such that when discovered the reptile is as likely as not to attack. It is responsible for the majority of deaths from snakebite in Australia and Tasmania.

The tiger snake gets its name from the dark brown or blackish stripes on its tawny body. The head is usually dark. The snake prefers dry and brushy country where it feeds upon both warm- and cold-blooded prey, showing a preference for rats.

When excited the tiger snake raises the anterior part of its body into the air and spreads its neck somewhat as does the cobra, to which reptile it is related. From this position it strikes vigorously. The lunge carries the snake forward a little, then another strike follows, so that when thoroughly enraged the tiger snake appears to take short jumps at the object of its wrath.

The Death Adder

The death adder is another Australian snake that has a deservedly bad reputation. This snake also belongs to the cobra group, as do all the poisonous snakes of Australia. Its appearance is very viperlike, however, and so it is small wonder that it has been tagged with the popular name of "adder." It is short and rather squat with a large head. Its average length is less than two feet.

The snake is brownish or greenish in color with numerous dark cross-bands. It is a lover of dry and sandy places and is nocturnal in its habits. During the day it lies quietly among the grasses and weeds, often partly buried in the sand. Its coloration so closely matches that of its surroundings that there is great danger of stepping on a specimen before it is seen. Herein lies the chief danger from this reptile, for it is not aggressive and does not fly into a rage when cornered, as does the tiger snake just described. While records of bites by this snake are not so common as those by the tiger snake, the percentage of fatalities is just as high, fully 50 per cent of those bitten failing to recover.

The death adder gives birth to living young, the litters averaging about twelve.

The Australian Blacksnake

The Australian blacksnake is another poisonous species that plagues the inhabitants of the continent "Down Under," but this one is not nearly so dangerous as the two just discussed. Being a very abundant reptile, probably more people are bitten by it than by any other Australian venomous snake. Fortunately, however, its venom is not very powerful and deaths from the bite of the blacksnake are rare.

This species is built along the general lines of an American racer; it is trim but sturdy. Its length is between five and six feet, and its color a rich bluish black on the back, while on the sides the scales are edged with scarlet. The underside is red and black. The scales being smooth, the reptile has a satiny appearance. Though able to flatten its neck to some extent, it has no real hood.

Although the Australian blacksnake is to be found in a variety of locations, it shows a preference for marshy country. It enters the water freely and swims well. It feeds upon small mammals and birds, lizards and small snakes, and is very fond of frogs. When on the defensive it does not rear up as the cobra does, but often lifts its head a few inches from the ground as it faces its disturber. The Australian blacksnake produces living young, usually about twenty at a time.

The Common Viper

This snake is very widely distributed throughout Europe and Asia. It occurs in the British Isles, where it has the distinction of being Britain's only venomous serpent. It is also found over much of central and northern Europe, across Asia into Siberia, and is present on several of the islands north of Japan. Its range extends farther north than that of any other poisonous snake.

A stockily built reptile, it is not so fat, sluggish, and big-headed as many of the African members of the viper clan. The color is variable, as one would expect with such a widely distributed species, but it is commonly greenish gray with a dark zigzag band down the center of the back. Some specimens may be deep brownish black, others pale pinkish gray, but the darker zigzag longitudinal band is fairly characteristic of the species. The lower surface is blackish, the scales are keeled. The viper's average length is about two feet.

As a rule this reptile prefers open country. It is ordinarily found in briar fields, in weedy corners of stone piles or quarries, and along the borders of cultivated fields. It is a strictly terrestrial snake. It does not willingly enter the water, nor does it do any climbing of trees. In the late summer it is often encountered in cornfields, where it searches for mice under the shocks of grain. The snake loves to bask in the sun, and is frequently seen contentedly coiled

(New York Zoological Society Photo)

EUROPEAN VIPER
Greenish gray, with a dark zigzag band on the back.

atop some flat rock in an exposed position. Aside from these sun baths the snake is essentially nocturnal.

The common viper feeds chiefly upon mice. It is reported as a difficult species to keep successfully in captivity, most individuals refusing to accept food and ultimately starving to death. The young, which are born alive, generally come in large broods. The venom of this snake, while poisonous, is rarely fatal to man. It is well adapted, however, for paralyzing the small prey upon which the adder subsists.

RUSSELL'S VIPER

Russell's viper is a deadly reptile living throughout much of the Far East where it ably assists the cobra in establishing an abnormally high death rate among the native population. Its venom is not so potent as that of the cobra, but the snake has the long fangs of the vipers and it can inject a large dose deep into the tissues of the

RUSSELL'S VIPER—INDIA
Pale gray, with brown spots that are edged with black.

bitten victim. Russell's viper occurs in southern India and Ceylon, in southern Burma, Thailand, and Java.

This serpent averages a little under four feet in length, but some specimens attain a length of more than five feet. It is a rather stout reptile, likely to have the greatest body circumference of any Aisatic snake except, of course, the pythons. The head is heavy and flat and distinctly triangular in outline. The scales are strongly keeled.

The coloration is quite striking. The ground color is usually pale sandy gray and there are three series of large, rounded spots extending down the back. These spots, chocolate brown rimmed with black, are often bordered with white or yellow. Frequently two or more spots fuse to form a partial chainlike pattern. The lower surface is yellowish with scattered dark markings. Throughout much of its range this snake is called the *tic-polonga,* which is Sinhalese for "spotted snake."

Russell's viper prefers open country and is not often found in dense jungles. Its habits are largely nocturnal. Those individuals that are found during the day are usually resting, coiled up and fairly well concealed by the tall grass. It is not a particularly bad-tempered reptile, and collectors report that it commonly shows a reluctance to bite, contenting itself with hissing violently when disturbed and refusing to strike unless considerably irritated. There is a case on record where a hunter carried one of these deadly vipers for miles, with no precautions whatever, under the impression that he had captured a baby python! When he reached camp his "python" promptly bit a dog which died within ten minutes. Despite the usually lazy actions of Russell's viper, it can be so thoroughly enraged that it will fairly hurl itself at its enemy.

This snake feeds principally upon small mammals, with rats probably constituting the bulk of its prey. It will eat lizards, however, and captive specimens will readily accept frogs and other snakes. As a matter of fact Russell's viper is reputedly one of the easiest of all venomous snakes to satisfy so far as the food problem is concerned. The young, which are born alive, average about ten inches in length at birth. Russell's viper is a very prolific species, often producing fifty or more at a time.

The Puff Adder

This is probably the best known viper in Africa, and certainly the most widely distributed. It occurs in most parts of that continent except the extreme north, and it is to be found in Arabia as well. A very stout-bodied reptile, it averages about four feet in length. It is extremely deadly.

The general ground color is buffy gray, heavily speckled with white. The back bears a series of black, crescent-shaped marks, each bordered at the rear with creamy yellow. These crescents merge into bands toward the tail. The head is broad and flat and thoroughly viperlike in appearance.

When disturbed this serpent faces its enemy and takes an enormous breath which inflates the body noticeably. The air is then expelled with a loud and prolonged hiss, after which the snake repeats the performance. This trait is characteristic of many of the vipers and is responsible for the name "puff adder" being applied to this common species.

This snake inhabits dry, semiarid locations, keeping pretty well out of sight during the daytime and doing its prowling after dark. It feeds chiefly upon rodents which it captures by lying motionless along trails and runways, often half buried in the sand.

The Gaboon Viper

When we see the word "viper" we usually think of a short, fat, thick-bodied, big-headed snake. The gaboon viper fits this conception perfectly. Averaging only about three feet in length, its diameter at the thickest part may be nearly eight inches. The head is tremendously large and sinister looking, while at the other end the bloated body tapers very abruptly to a ridiculously short tail. The serpent's home is in tropical Africa where it occurs from coast to coast.

The markings on this snake are rich and decorative, but hard to describe. The back bears a bewildering pattern of elongate bars, rhombs, and crescents, while the sides are decorated with hourglass marks and half-diamonds. The colors involved are chocolate, buff, purplish, and brown. The broad head is pale brown with a heavy black line under each eye.

The gaboon viper is a reptile of the jungles, making its home in the moist, forested areas where its bizarre markings blend surprisingly well with its surroundings. It commonly lies concealed among the ferns and vines on the jungle floor waiting the approach of some unsuspecting bird or rodent. The snake rarely makes any attempt to escape when discovered, but merely assumes a defensive position and by hissing repeatedly warns you to keep your distance. One look at this three-foot snake with a head as big as that of a fifteen-foot python, and one doesn't need to be a snake expert to know that here is a reptile to leave strictly alone! It is one of the most deadly of all known snakes.

THE RHINOCEROS VIPER

Another heavy-bodied, awesome-looking reptile, this one living in tropical West Africa, is the rhinoceros viper. This snake, which averages less than three feet in length, is not so stout as the gaboon viper just described, nor is its head so large in proportion. The head of this snake, however, is even more bizarre, for it bears two large horns on the nose and there may be several smaller ones as well. The scales are very strongly keeled.

This is another gorgeously colored reptile when freshly shed. The ground color is olive gray. On the back there is a series of elongate blue patches, each rimmed with yellow and set in a black diamond. Large reddish triangles adorn the sides, while the head is bluish with a black lance-shaped mark that points forward. The horns are yellow. All in all the colors and pattern of this serpent actually appear to be artificial. They are at their best only directly after shedding has taken place, after which they soon become dull and indistinct.

This reptile's habits are quite different from those of most of the other vipers. Instead of haunting dry and sandy territory, the rhinoceros viper leads a semiaquatic life. Its home is along river banks where it finds an abundance of food in the form of rodents and birds. The snake is almost as good a swimmer as a typical water snake.

The rhinoceros viper is regarded as an extremely dangerous reptile. Owing to its general preference for the banks of streams it is popularly known as the "River Jack."

THE BUSHMASTER

The bushmaster is the largest poisonous snake of the New World. Its home is in South and Central America, and its maximum length is between eleven and twelve feet, although the average specimen is less than eight feet long. It is a pit viper, a strong and robust snake, but rather slender in build.

The ground color is pinkish yellow or pinkish gray, and the upper surface is decorated with large black patches that are wide on the back and narrowed to a point on the sides so that in effect they are diamond-shaped. The scales are strongly keeled, so strongly in fact that the reptile's body is almost spiny; the skin has been likened to the surface of a pineapple. The tail ends in a hard and sharp spine.

The bushmaster is essentially a forest snake; it is seldom found in open country. Many of the specimens discovered have been located in the entrances of underground burrows of jungle animals, apparently favorite spots for this snake to spend the day in. The bushmaster's large size is fully backed up by enormously developed fangs. The reptile's venom is as toxic as that of any pit viper, so in South America it is generally considered *the* snake to be feared. Fortunately it is not very common, and its choice of country is such that relatively few specimens are ever seen.

Despite the bushmaster's large size and quite evident ability to take care of itself in jungle warfare, it appears to be very delicate in captivity. Very few individuals are captured alive, and the occasional specimens that eventually arrive at our zoological parks seldom live more than a few months. In almost every case they have stubbornly refused to accept food. It is interesting to note that the bushmaster lays eggs because it is the only New World pit viper that does so. All the others produce living young.

THE FER-DE-LANCE

The fer-de-lance is another dreaded snake of tropical America, but while the bushmaster is relatively rare this one is quite common. It occurs from southern Mexico to the south of Brazil. It is a large, moderately slender snake, attaining a length of slightly more than eight feet. An average specimen measures between five and six feet.

It is a variable snake in coloration, but it generally has a rich, well-marked pattern. The ground color may be gray or olive or reddish, and the sides are decorated with a series of large, dark triangles whose points meet on the snake's back. The triangles, edged with white, give the reptile a very striking appearance. The chin and throat are commonly tinged with yellow or orange. The head is large and distinctly lance-shaped.

The fer-de-lance is not restricted to any one kind of territory. It is equally at home in marshy country and in dry hilly regions. It is usually more abundant in the neighborhood of plantations than it is in wilder sections, no doubt being drawn to such places by the prevalence of rodents which form the major item on the snake's bill of fare.

The fer-de-lance, which is very deadly, is beyond doubt the most dangerous snake likely to be encountered in tropical America. As mentioned above, it is likely to be rather common on sugar planta-tions. In the hope of reducing its numbers, the Indian mongoose, a noted cobra killer, was introduced several years ago. The cobra strikes a relatively slow, downward blow from a raised position. The agile mongoose has little trouble in dodging this strike and sinking its sharp teeth into the snake's skull before it can recover. The fer-de-lance, however, strikes from a coiled or partially coiled position, its strike being horizontal as well as lightning fast. Against this type of fighting the mongoose was no match for the pit viper, so it very wisely left the reptile strictly alone. Today the introduced mongoose is thriving in its new home, feeding chiefly upon the natives' poultry and the small game of the country. It has become a first-rate pest as well as a monumental example of the danger involved in introducing any foreign animal without proper study of its habits.

Unlike the bushmaster, the fer-de-lance does very well in cap-tivity. It accepts food readily and appears to stand confinement better than many of the other pit vipers. The young are born alive. Broods are large, often from fifty to sixty, a factor that contrib-utes to the snake's continued moderate abundance over a wide territory.

The South American Rattlesnake

South of Mexico we find but two species of rattlesnake, although the common one is divided into three subspecies. Together they range from Central America to well down into South America. A typical specimen is marked somewhat like our Florida diamondback, but is generally less vividly colored. It differs from our rattler by having a pair of broad black stripes on its head and neck, one on each side. The reptile is about five feet long and rather stocky in build. It has keeled scales.

Called the *cascabel* (little bell) in Spanish, this serpent lives in the dry hilly country and generally avoids the swampy tropical lowlands. Its habits are about the same as those of the rattlesnakes of more northern latitudes, its prey being made up largely of warm-blooded animals, with rodents constituting the major part. As with the other rattlesnakes, the young are born alive.

Throughout South America this snake is rightfully regarded as being very dangerous. Although it is a typical pit viper, its venom has some of the properties of that usually associated with the cobra group in that it attacks the nerve centers as well as the red blood cells. It is regarded as being extraordinarily potent. In addition to its venom and the long fangs for injecting it, the snake is usually very bad natured; it often strikes without bothering to rattle. If it is teased a little, it does not hesitate to attack its tormentor, something the northern rattlesnakes are seldom if ever known to do.

The Palm Viper

The palm vipers are big-headed snakes with relatively small bodies. There are a number of species living chiefly in Central America, and none of them get to be much over two feet in length.

These serpents, which are expert climbers, are usually found among the branches and fronds of the luxuriant tropical foliage. They are by no means confined to palm trees, although they are reported commonly to coil where the base of a palm stem joins the trunk. The snake's tail, which is prehensile, is usually wrapped tightly around a branch.

Probably the best known species is the horned palm viper, a moderately slender snake with a head that appears two or three sizes too big for its body. There is a prominent spiny horn over each eye. The color is rather variable and there appear to be two main phases: one is olive green spotted with red and black, the other is pale yellow speckled with black. This species ranges through most of Central America and well down into northern South America.

Though the palm vipers (which are not true vipers but pit vipers) are small snakes, they have very large fangs and their venom is extremely poisonous. In some ways they are more dangerous than the much larger ground-dwelling pit vipers for they are usually encountered in thick jungle foliage and are commonly just at the strategic height for striking a person in the face or on the neck.

THE SEA SNAKES

Old seafaring men used to regale the credulous with tales about sea serpents that they had allegedly seen on their voyages around the world. Though these mythical monsters, usually many feet long and with more or less dragonlike heads, have long since been relegated to their rightful place with other fairy stories of earlier days, nevertheless we *do* have sea serpents! The largest of them (about nine feet long), however, could hardly be responsible for the startling and fanciful tales that added spice to life at sea a few generations ago.

These are the sea snakes, living their whole lives in salt water. They are believed to have developed from the cobra group. Though all of them are highly venomous, accidents involving sea snakes are not common. This type of reptile has become thoroughly adapted for marine life. The body is compressed from side to side, the tail is flattened to form a most efficient oarlike appendage, and the snake has developed valves that close its throat and nostrils completely. Sea snakes are confined to the Indian and Pacific oceans. One species crosses the Pacific and occurs on the coasts of South

America and Mexico. Sea snakes are entirely absent from the Atlantic Ocean.

From our viewpoint the best known member of this interesting group is the yellow-bellied sea snake. This is a relatively small species, about three feet in length, which enjoys a very wide distribution. It is found from Australia to India, around most of the islands of the South Pacific, and on the western coast of the Americas from Ecuador to the Gulf of California.

The colors of this snake are quite variable. It may be black on the back and brown on the belly, with a bright yellow stripe separating the two colors, or it may be black above and yellow below, with no side stripe. The tail is often spotted or banded with yellow and black.

Although deadly poisonous the sea snakes are not aggressive. Fishermen of Indian Ocean ports are said to handle them with their bare hands when throwing them out of their nets, the larger ones being saved for food. Since sea snakes apparently never attack bathers, swimmers in the Orient do not hesitate to dive into waters known to harbor them in large numbers.

Sea snakes feed entirely upon fish, some of them confining their prey chiefly to eels. Observers have noted sea snakes lying motionless on the water, apparently simulating a floating stick. Small fish often huddle near floating objects, such as branches, twigs, and seaweed, probably for protection. When a few have gathered about the sea snake, it makes a sudden lunge and captures one.

Sea snakes are about as nocturnal as they are diurnal. They are likely to be seen at any time of day, and are attracted by lights suspended near the water at night. They are perhaps most abundant just off river mouths, probably because the hunting for small fish is superior in such places.

The only occasion when sea snakes come ashore is when it is time for egg laying. Then they resort to some rocky island and manage to climb about over the slippery rocks. Once the eggs are laid the snakes go back to their marine life, and as soon as the baby sea snakes are hatched they too drop into the sea and begin their completely marine existence.

Chapter 10

THE CARE AND FEEDING OF SNAKES

Very few people would even dream of keeping a snake around the house. Yet there are those who like to have some living thing to care for and study, and for such persons the snake offers some advantages over the more usual type of pet. Let us consider a few of these advantages.

In the first place, reptiles do not require a great deal of room. Several may be kept in a relatively small space, and they do not need to be "taken for a walk" periodically! Snakes are remarkably quiet. Even the most ardent bird lovers occasionally get a little tired of the incessant singing of a vigorous canary, and if a near neighbor happens to be a person who doesn't particularly enjoy the chirps and trills of our yellow-feathered friend, it can be a real nuisance to him. Cats mew and occasionally yowl, and dogs whine and bark. A collection of snakes, however, will never cause any complaints from neighbors on the ground of noise.

Reptiles require an absolute minimum of care. If you are going away for the week end, or for a week or ten days at the seashore, you have to make some arrangements with a friend for feeding and caring for your dog or cat, parrot or canary, or even for your goldfish. But not for your snakes. Serpents fast for days, by choice, and if you make certain that your pets have provisions for drinking, you can safely leave them without care until you get back.

Of course no snake will ever show affection for its keeper, like a dog will, but neither will a goldfish. Many a snake can be tamed. It will show surprising traits after you have really become acquainted with it and the snake has become accustomed to you.

Those young people who are interested, and who are inclined to study snakes, can profit by keeping a few in captivity. Many interesting facts about the reptile's habits are thus placed before your very eyes. You can observe the manner of feeding as well as the snake's method of overpowering struggling prey, its manner of progression and tree climbing, its way of getting rid of its epidermis, and numberless other things that are rarely to be observed about snakes in a wild state.

The first thing to decide on is a suitable cage. From the standpoint of an animal there is no such thing as a perfect cage, but from your own viewpoint there are several things to consider. First of all it must be escape-proof, or you will be very unpopular with your neighbors! It is to be understood that these suggestions for snake rearing apply *only* to nonvenomous, harmless snakes. No poisonous snake should ever be kept alive by any but an experienced person, and then only in proper places, such as institutions and zoological parks, not in neighborhood back yards. Snakes are expert at finding some loose section of screening or a weak corner of their cage, and it is astonishing what a small crack one can squeeze through. So make certain, first of all, that your cage is escape-proof.

Most snake enthusiasts favor a rectangular box with a glass front and a wire (hardware cloth) top. The top, which affords entrance to the cage, may be hinged or sliding. Most snake keepers prefer the sliding top. Either one is better than a side door which swings open, as too many snakes escape while the keeper is opening the door. The upper part of the back should be of wire (hardware cloth) in order to provide additional ventilation. An easily constructed cage that anyone able to use saw and hammer can build with little trouble is shown herewith. For ease of cleaning, an important item, the glass front should be removable. With a little extra work you can provide your cage with a sliding metal floor.

The size will depend on what kind of snakes you intend to keep. For a garter snake, a hog-nosed snake, or any other species that is only a little more than two feet long, dimensions of 15 inches by 24 inches, with a height of 15 inches, will be ample. A cage as small as 8 inches by 12 inches by 8 inches is large enough for DeKay's snake, ring-necks, or smooth green snakes, while for the larger blacksnakes, rat snakes, and king snakes one needs a cage about 18 inches by 36 inches by 20 inches. Your snake needs room enough to crawl about freely, and the height should be sufficient for the inmate to crawl vertically as well as horizontally.

You can dress up the interior of your cage according to your own ideas, bearing in mind the habits of the snake you intend to keep in it. Most important is the water dish. This should be large

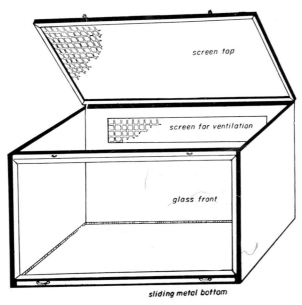

Typical snake cage.

enough for the snake to coil in, for many varieties like to soak themselves for hours at a time. Dishes of glass or crockery are preferable to metal ones, and they should be securely wedged in one corner of the cage in such a way that there is no chance of its being overturned by the snake. The water dish should be kept clean and at all times filled with clean water.

You will want your specimens out in the open where you and your friends can see them, but it is wise to provide a retreat of some sort where the snake can go for a rest. Remember the snake has no movable eyelids and that it can rest (sleep?) only where it can get into a dark or dimly lighted place. A flat stone, wedged up a little on one side with a pebble or two, or a rough slab of bark to crawl under, will do nicely for small reptiles, but for larger ones a small box with an opening at one end should be provided. This may be an old cardboard shoe box, or some other container that can be replaced as it gets soiled. A short section of a hollow log makes a splendid retreat but it is rather hard to keep clean.

Many snakes like to climb. For these install a short section of tree, with several sawed-off branches. This will provide a roving ground as well as a resting place for your pets and will teach you much about how these legless and handless creatures manage to

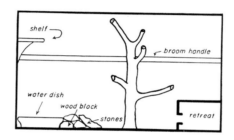

Arrangement of cage interior.

scale considerable heights. A small shelf bracketed against one end of the cage, near the top, will be utilized a good share of the time, and a broom handle or similar rod, stretched directly across the cage, will give you an opportunity to watch many examples of reptilian gymnastics. The accompanying diagram will give you an idea of this sort of arrangement in a snake cage.

Cleanliness is of paramount importance, as it is with any kind of pet housing. The cage should be cleaned regularly, and occasionally taken apart and scrubbed with a weak ammonia solution. Special care should be taken to see that the water dish and the retreat are clean at all times.

The most difficult part of snake raising is in getting your pets to eat. Some varieties, such as garter snakes, hog-nosed snakes, and water snakes, usually accept food rather quickly, while others, such as blacksnakes and milk snakes, commonly refuse to eat. All snakes are carnivorous and all of them ordinarily eat food that they kill themselves. After a snake has been in captivity for some time, and has eaten regularly, it can often be induced to accept a dead mouse, bird, or fish, or even a strip of beef, especially if it is offered on the end of a wire or stick and kept in motion until the snake grabs it. It is usually futile, however, to offer dead food to a freshly captured snake.

Some people will object to giving live animals to a captive snake, on the grounds of cruelty. The eating habits of all carnivorous animals are necessarily cruel, even the cat's by your fireside or the robin's in your orchard. There is probably no quicker or more merciful death than that of a mouse attacked by a constricting snake. The rodent is seen sniffing curiously at the serpent, showing no signs of panic or fear, when suddenly the reptile strikes and the mouse practically disappears from view, concealed in the snake's coils. Death is almost instantaneous and it is certain that the mouse never knows what hits him. Certainly the rodent suffers less than if it had been struck over the head with a stick and then offered to the snake.

Snakes do not need to eat very often. A meal once a week is enough for most, and many are satisfied with one every two weeks. The smaller varieties that eat earthworms and insects can be fed every few days. There is no danger of overfeeding for the snake can be depended upon to stop when it has had enough.

The food, according to what kind of snake you have, should be put in the cage at dusk and left overnight. Snakes are much more likely to eat when things are quiet and when they are not closely watched. If in the morning the food has not been taken, remove it, wait a couple of days, then try the snake with it again.

If your snake refuses to eat after several attempts on your part to provide it with a meal, you will have to try force-feeding. This is not so difficult as it may sound. You simply pick the reptile up, holding it just back of the head, and force its mouth open. A bit of meat or a piece of fish or frog is then gently but firmly forced down the snake's throat. Dipping the food in cod-liver oil will help and will do the snake no harm. But do not use large pieces of food, even though the snake's throat is quite elastic.

With the food part way down the reptile's throat, give him a chance to swallow voluntarily. If he refuses to cooperate, simply massage the lump gently, rubbing it above and away from the snake's head until it goes down. Repeat this operation until you think your pet has had a substantial meal. During the times when natural food was hard to get, the writer had good results by purchasing large gelatin capsules from the drugstore, filling them with hamburger meat, and forcing them down the throats of his reluctant snakes. Most specimens will accept food after a few force-feedings, although some individuals are more stubborn than others.

Following is a list of common, nonpoisonous snakes that are recommended for the beginner in snake culture, with suggestions as to the preferred food of each.

Garter Snakes	Earthworms, small frogs
Water Snake	Frogs, fish
Ribbon Snake	Small frogs, tadpoles
DeKay's Snake	Worms, salamanders
Ring-Necked Snake	Worms, salamanders, insects
Green Snake	Worms, insects, grubs
Hog-Nosed Snake	Toads
Blacksnake	Mice, frogs
Rat Snake	Rodents, lizards, eggs
King Snake	Small snakes, lizards, mice
Milk Snake	Mice
Corn Snake	Mice, rats
Bull Snake	Rats, small rabbits

Every few weeks your snakes will cast their skins. The time between sheddings varies considerably; some snakes only go through the process two or three times a year, while others may shed every month or so. The first sign that shedding is near comes when your snake's eyes become clouded, and take on a bluish white appearance as though the reptile were going blind. The snake acts listless, and is frequently irritable, and refuses to eat. After a time the serpent will be noted rubbing its chin vigorously against a stone, or a branch. Finally the skin breaks at this point and your pet literally crawls out of it, turning it inside out as it goes. If there are plenty of stones, twigs, and other rough surfaces in the cage for the snake to crawl and rub against, it should have no difficulty, but sometimes captive snakes require a little assistance. If the old skin sticks in places, especially around the head, it may be necessary to soak the snake in water for a brief period and then use a pair of tweezers for removing the stubborn patches. Most snakes are surprisingly docile and tolerant while you are working at this job. After the shedding has been completed your pet will be at its very best both in shining colors and in all-round alertness, and it will usually be ready for a meal.

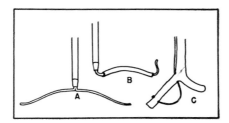

Collecting sticks.

The snake enthusiast will not have to be told where to obtain material. He will be familiar with the various fields and swamp-lands of his neighborhood, and the discussions of various harmless snakes in this book will offer many suggestions about where to look for the various species.

Three types of collecting stick are shown in the illustration, al-though many boys will prefer to collect their subjects barehanded. The old-fashioned forked stick is not to be trusted on uneven, stony ground. *A* shows a more efficient type which can be used on any kind of ground, the object being, of course, to pin the snake down so you can grasp it by its neck and thus avoid being bitten. If a short section of rubber tubing is put on over the metal prongs, there is less chance of injuring the captive. If you should have your snake pinned down by its middle, release the pressure a little and it will attempt to move forward. If you prevent this by pressing on your stick, after a few attempts the snake will try backing up. Then, when it has squirmed backwards until the prongs are just above its neck, press down and you have it. *B* shows a stick that can be used in the same way or in guiding or otherwise controlling a serpent's movements. *C* is a homemade device for capturing larger snakes, including the dangerous ones. Its use is self-explanatory.

You can keep more than one snake, or more than one species of snake, in the same cage, provided that you use a little care and thought in your selection. Some species like nothing better than to eat other snakes, so you must be careful to keep these kinds separate. In this connection the chief ones to watch are the king snakes, gopher snakes, milk snakes, and the blacksnakes. The king snake will sometimes kill and manage to swallow another snake actually larger than itself.

Treat your snakes with consideration. Try to think of them as your guests rather than your captives. Once you have taken them from their wild haunts they are your responsibility. They like a warm environment, but it is a mistake to keep them in bright sunshine for lengthy periods. Remember that the sun, shining against the glass front of a cage, can build up a terrific heat inside. So see to it that part of your cage is in the shade. Try to keep the temperature under 80° Fahrenheit.

Thoughtless persons sometimes wave their hands about close to the glass front in order to tease the snake into striking at the glass. Freshly caught snakes, especially water snakes and blacksnakes, will strike savagely when so tormented, and it doesn't take long for one to develop a first-rate bruise on its nose. It goes without saying that if you intend to tame your snakes you will stand for none of this cruel treatment.

To begin with, you should handle your snake by holding it just back of the jaws so that it cannot bite. Always approach the snake from above, never from the reptile's own level, and always keep your movements slow and deliberate, never quick or jerky. After a while the snake will begin to realize that it is not going to be hurt when it is picked up, and it will struggle less and less. After the snake has learned this lesson you can safely release the neck hold and permit the serpent to crawl through your fingers. In a surprisingly short time it will show no evidence of fear or anger when you pick it up, and it may even seem to enjoy being handled.

In the temperate zone snakes hibernate during the cold months. If you can maintain an even temperature in the room where the cages are kept, the occupants will remain more or less active all winter, although they may act torpid at times and refuse to eat regularly. Maintaining a proper temperature, however, is much easier than maintaining a constant supply of food during the winter months, especially for those varieties that eat frogs, toads, and insects. It is therefore advisable, in most cases, to start your "snake farm" in the spring, enjoy it all summer, and then release your specimens by early October while there is still time for them to seek a safe refuge for hibernation. One word of warning. Do not release any specimen that is not native to your part of the country. If you have a southern rat snake, for instance, do not turn it loose in Massachusetts!

LIST OF AUTHORITIES CITED

Following is a list of men who have been mentioned several times throughout this book, particularly in statements regarding the length of some serpents. This is in no sense to be regarded as a complete list of American herpetologists, since many of our most respected authorities are not recorded here.

1. Amaral, Afranio do. A South American herpetologist who is noted for his work on snake poisons.
2. Bailey, Vernon (1864-1944). Late Chief Field Naturalist of the Bureau of Biological Survey of the United States Department of Agriculture.
3. Baird, Spencer F. (1823-1887). At one time secretary of the Smithsonian Institution, he was very active in describing new species of animals at the time when our western states were first being explored. Together with Charles Girard (one of his students) and Robert Kennicott, Baird added fifty-seven species of snakes to our national list.
4. Blanchard, Frank N. (1888-1937). A noted zoologist at the University of Michigan. Author of *A Revision of the King Snakes,* Bulletin No. 114 of the United States National Museum.
5. Conant, Roger (1909-   ). Curator of reptiles at the Philadelphia Zoological Garden. Author of *Reptiles of Ohio* and many other works on snakes and other reptiles. Co-author, with William Bridges, of *What Snake Is That?*
6. Cope, Edward D. (1840-1897). A pioneer naturalist with the Philadelphia Academy and later at Princeton University. He was the author of many monumental works on reptiles and fishes, and is especially noted for his studies of fossil forms.
7. *Copeia,* a quarterly journal, is the official organ of the American Society of Icthyologists and Herpetologists. Edward Raney, of Cornell University, is secretary of the organization.
8. Ditmars, Raymond L. (1876-1942). Late curator of reptiles and mammals at the New York Zoological Society. He was author of *The Reptile Book* and many other popular and learned treatises on snakes and other animals.
9. Klauber, Laurence M. (1883-   ). Curator of reptiles of the Zoological Society of San Diego. He is a distinguished authority on American rattlesnakes.
10. Pack, Herbert J. In *Copeia,* No. 68 (1919).

175

11. Smith, Hobart M. (1912-   ). A herpetologist at the University of Illinois. Author of a *Handbook of Lizards* and of many works on snakes.

12. Stejneger, Leonard H. (1851-1943). Late curator of reptiles at the United States National Museum. Co-author (with the late Thomas Barbour of the Museum of Comparative Zoology of Harvard University) of the *Check List of North American Amphibians and Reptiles.*

BOOKS FOR FURTHER READING

Below is a selected list of books recommended to those readers who may wish to follow the interesting study of snakes still further. Many of these books contain extensive bibliographies, including county and state lists for all sections of this country.

Barbour, Thomas. *Reptiles and Amphibians: Their Habits and Adaptations.* Boston, Houghton Mifflin Co., 1934.

Conant, Roger. *Reptile Study* (Merit Badge Series). New York, Boy Scouts of America, 1944.

Conant, Roger, and Bridges, William. *What Snake Is That?* New York, D. Appleton-Century Co., 1939.

Curran, Charles H., and Kauffeld, Carl. *Snakes and Their Ways.* New York, Harper & Bros., 1937.

Ditmars, Raymond L. *A Field Book of North American Snakes.* New York, Doubleday, Doran & Co., 1939.

Ditmars, Raymond L. *Reptiles of North America.* New York, Doubleday, Doran & Co., 1936.

Ditmars, Raymond L. *Reptiles of the World.* New York, The Macmillan Co., 1928.

Gloyd, Howard. *The Rattlesnakes.* Chicago Academy of Sciences, Special Publication No. 4, 1940.

Morris, P. A. *They Hop and Crawl.* New York, The Ronald Press Co., 1944.

Pickwell, Gale. *Amphibians and Reptiles of the Pacific States.* Stanford University Press, 1947.

Pope, Clifford H. *Snakes Alive and How They Live.* New York, The Viking Press, 1937.

Pope, Clifford H. *The Poisonous Snakes of the New World.* New York Zoological Society, 1944.

Schmidt, Karl P., and Davis, Delbert D. *Field Book of Snakes of the United States and Canada.* New York, G. P. Putnam's Sons, 1941.

Stejneger, Leonard H., and Barbour, Thomas. *Check List of North American Amphibians and Reptiles.* (5th ed.) Bulletin of the Museum of Comparative Zoology, Cambridge, Harvard University Press, 1943.

CLASSIFICATION OF SNAKES MENTIONED
IN THIS BOOK

UNITED STATES SNAKES

FAMILY LEPTOTYPHLOPIDAE

179

FAMILY ELAPIDAE

FAMILY CROTALIDAE

FOREIGN SNAKES

FAMILY BOIDAE

FAMILY COLUBRIDAE

FAMILY HYDROPHIIDAE

INDEX